Philosophy and Human Geography

An Introduction to Contemporary Approaches

R. J. Johnston

Professor of Geography, University of Sheffield

Edward Arnold

Copyright © 1983 R. J. Johnston

First published in Great Britain 1983 by
Edward Arnold (Publishers) Ltd,
41 Bedford Square, London WC1B 3DQ

Edward Arnold (Australia) Pty Ltd, 80 Waverley Road, Caulfield East, Victoria 3145, Australia

Edward Arnold, 300 North Charles Street, Baltimore, Maryland 21201, U.S.A.

Reprinted 1984

British Library Cataloguing in Publication Data

Johnston, Ronald J.
  Philosophy and human geography.
  1. Anthropo-geography 2. Anthropo-geography—Philosophy
  I. Title
  909   GF21

ISBN 0 7131 6385 2

All rights reserved. No part of this publication may be reproduced, stored in a retrieval system, or transmitted in any form or by any means, electronic, photocopying, recording, or otherwise, without the prior permission of Edward Arnold (Publishers) Ltd.

Text set in 11/12 pt Bembo
(Compugraphic) by Colset Private Limited, Singapore.
Printed and bound in Great Britain by
Richard Clay (The Chaucer Press) Ltd, Bungay, Suffolk.

Contents

Preface — vi

1 Human geography — 1

The topical content of human geography – Elements of a philosophy of human geography – The development of human geography – The subdivisions of human geography – Summary

2 Positivist approaches — 11

The fundamentals of positivist science and of logical positivism – The methodology of positivism – Positivist social science – Positivism and human geography – The content of positivist human geography – Summary

3 Humanistic approaches — 52

Varieties of humanistic research – Humanistic approaches in human geography – Humanistic geography – An evaluation

4 Structuralist approaches — 87

Structure as construct – Structure as process – Structuralism in human geography – Structuralist geography – Summary

5 Conflict and accommodation — 122

Three geographies? – Integration? – Conclusion

Bibliography — 135

General index — 147

Index to authors — 150

Preface

Human geography is currently characterized by a great deal of lively debate which focuses not so much on its subject matter as on its philosophy: its orientation to its subject matter. Much more than was so in previous decades, human geographers are being exposed to debates within philosophy as they refer to the natural and, in particular, the social sciences. The foundations of geographical study are being excavated with questions such as 'What are the goals of human geographical research?', 'How can these be achieved?', 'What does pursuit of these goals imply with regard to the nature of evidence?' and so on. No longer can human geographers sit aside from such questions by offering themselves as the presenters of 'mere facts' – such things do not exist, the critics argue.

The present book has been designed as a companion to an earlier volume which traced the debates within human geography since 1945 over philosophical and methodological issues. In *Geography and Geographers: Anglo-American Human Geography since 1945* (Johnston, 1979 and 1983a), I showed how those debates covered the replacement of an empiricist philosophy by one that was positivist and how, in turn, the latter perspective was challenged by individuals of humanistic and of structuralist persuasions. The aim there was to examine the contemporary pluralism within the discipline rather than to explicate the details of the various philosophies. Here, the task is the complementary one of introducing the nature of the various philosophies with little reference to the debates over the relevance and validity of each.

The preface to that earlier book on the 'contemporary history' of human geography argued that students of the discipline need an understanding of why the content of their discipline is as it is and require a framework within which their own perspective can be developed. A similar case is made for the present book. In a discipline characterized by competition between a variety of philosophies, students need an introduction to those philosophies, a statement of their fundamentals and of their relevance to human geography. Such an introduction can be provided in a variety of ways. That chosen here is perhaps the simplest. The introductory chapter suggests that three competing philosophies (termed approaches here because each embraces a variety of related viewpoints) dominate contemporary human geography.

Preface vii

Each of the next three chapters takes one of these approaches and outlines its basic characteristics and use in human geography. Finally, the last chapter looks at attempts to link those approaches.

As an outline of the philosophy of social science, this book is very much a primer, a first statement. It does not pursue any topic in depth, and certainly does not offer a detailed explanation of any philosophies from which a reader could go away feeling schooled in the relevant approaches. The literature on these philosophies is extremely large: much of it, including some written specifically for geographers, is difficult, especially to the uninitiated. All that is attempted here is an introduction to the nature of the philosophies which human geographers are now exploring; any student wishing to join that quest will need to read a great deal more. Here, much of the discussion relies on secondary sources, so that the presentation has passed through several lenses before reaching the present pages, with all the potential for distortion that this implies. The main justification for this approach is that the secondary sources themselves isolate the main elements, whereas the primary works are in general too detailed – and often difficult. For a primer, succinctness and clarity are desirable; for later work in a philosophy, depth, detail and internal argument must also be explored.

As a primer directed at human geographers, this book does not seek to cover all philosophies. Nor are those included given the same amount of treatment. The general criterion determining the amount of coverage – within each of the three main chapters (2 to 4) – is the amount of use of the individual philosophy within human geography at the present time. Thus within the chapter on humanistic approaches, for example, existentialism is given less coverage than either idealism or phenomenology because it does not represent as substantial a part of the geographical literature. Such selectivity undoubtedly reflects some personal bias. It is not intended, however, to be prescriptive and to outline which are the better philosophies for geographers, or the better parts of particular philosophies (although some of the discussion in Chapter 5 refers to my attempts to integrate the various approaches). It is hoped that enough detail has been provided to indicate both the nature of each approach and its relevance to human geography – enough, that is, to stimulate the interested reader to investigate the topic further.

Like its companion, this book is in part based on the material presented in a final-year undergraduate course on the history and philosophy of contemporary human geography. As such, it assumes some knowledge of the substantive content of the discipline, some familiarity with its literature, and some experience of working (perhaps implicitly) within some of the approaches outlined here. For readers, it seeks to explicate the major features of the three sets of approaches, providing a foundation for understanding current philosophical debates in human geography, a basis for further exploration, and material on which they might base their own decisions about the proper approach to the discipline.

In producing this book, I am grateful to a number of people. My publishers prompted me to write it – leading me to read much more and to think many things through more fully than I had done previously; I, at least, have benefited from the project. Of my colleagues, Alan Hay has been a consistent focus of useful discussion and debate and I am extremely grateful to him for his continued intellectual companionship. Malcolm Lewis read through a complete draft, and made many useful suggestions which were very much appreciated; the usual disclaimer applies. My wife Rita also read a full draft and told me of the many places where I had not made things clear; I hope I have been able to improve them. Finally, I am once again in debt to Joan Dunn for her efficiency in translating handwritten manuscript into a final text.

1
Human geography

Within the academic community disciplines are almost invariably defined by their subject matter, by what it is that they study rather than how they study it. The boundaries between disciplines are rarely clearly delimited, however, because the reality that is being studied comprises an interrelated whole rather than a series of discrete parts. The division of knowledge into disciplines is therefore both artificial and, to a certain degree, arbitrary; the aim is to isolate certain topics that can be sensibly investigated separate from, though not independent of, others, although this ideal is not easily achieved. The boundaries are relatively porous, to allow for interdisciplinary contact, which increases as the volume of knowledge expands, and more specialized – yet at the same time less independent – disciplines are established to study particular topics.

From the above description, it could be deduced that the division of knowledge into academic disciplines is the result of logical decision-making and reflects the consensus of opinion of all those involved. This is far from the case. The academic division of labour at any one time is the result of earlier decisions that are difficult to overturn. Once established, a discipline not only marks out an intellectual territory but it becomes self-perpetuating; in particular it instructs students, who are socialized into that particular view of the world of learning and who propagate it. Attempts to change the division of labour, to create a new disciplinary structure, must therefore challenge the established orthodoxy, with all the potential dangers to personal status which such a conflict may generate. Some challenges succeed, but not necessarily everywhere, so that in different countries, and sometimes in the same country, the allocation of topics to disciplines may vary; in some cases, the successful challenges reflect the efforts of particular individuals who are able to establish new academic centres around themselves, perhaps to the detriment of one or more existing disciplines.

A discipline is brought into existence because those propagating it are able to show to potential sponsors that its topical content is worthy of study and that its means of study are valid. In the broadest sense therefore, a discipline has to demonstrate its utility. Once established, to some extent its utility will be self-generating. The discipline will need a continuing supply of researchers to provide new knowledge, for example, and a stream of trained teachers, to induct the next generations of students. Failure to maintain the support of sponsors may lead to disciplinary decline – perhaps at the expense of an expanding 'invader'. This too may be self-generating, for fewer students need fewer teachers and doubts about the discipline's utility may mean a falling demand for its research. Thus the established members of a discipline find it necessary to promote it. Such promotional activity is especially strong when resources are scarce and the potential for decline considerable.

Although to a considerable extent a discipline sells itself according to what it studies, it must also develop a philosophy regarding the orientation: how should it study its particular subject matter, and why? In some disciplines it may be argued that this is an irrelevant question, that there is only one possible philosophy. But in others this is not so, and there may be considerable debate on philosophical issues. To some extent this too revolves around questions of utility: which philosophy is best suited to the demands of the sponsors? (Not all academics subscribe to the view that they must orient their disciplines towards sponsors, who increasingly are governments. Some claim that they have a more correct interpretation of what is valuable and what is not, and interpret their function as convincing either the sponsors or society as a whole of the rightness of this interpretation.) It may well be, therefore, that within a discipline there is considerable debate about its conduct, which may focus not only on what should be done but on who the discipline should serve.

The preceding paragraphs suggest that the academic world comprises a series of disciplines, each occupying a niche within the structure of knowledge (but allowing a certain amount of light to filter in from adjacent niches). The nature of that niche has been created, and is continually being recreated, around a particular focus – the disciplinary subject matter. Within it, there may be considerable debate about how that subject matter should be studied, and to what ends. Human geography occupies one such niche, and it is currently experiencing major philosophical discussions. The aim of the present book is to provide a brief introduction to the foundations of those discussions by outlining the nature of the competing philosophies, the claims for them as valid approaches to human geography, and their contribution to the development of the discipline as a store of knowledge.

The topical content of human geography

Ever since its promulgation as a separate discipline in the nineteenth century, geography has had a twin focus on space and place. (For an outline history, see James and Martin, 1981.) At any location on the earth's surface (most geographers have concentrated on the land surface) there are both vertical and horizontal relationships: the vertical relationships link different elements in the same location, whereas the horizontal relationships link elements in separate locations. The relative importance of these two sets of relationships has varied over time, with geographers becoming increasingly concerned in recent decades with the horizontal (Cox, 1976). Many geographers stress that it is this twin focus, however, and even more so the integration of the two sets of relationships, that provides the discipline with its identity and integrity (see Haggett, 1980).

Within this academic niche, human geographers study only some of the relationships, leaving others to physical geographers. On the vertical theme, they investigate interrelationships between people and their environment (natural and man-made – some argue that the two cannot be separated). On the horizontal theme, they study inter-place interrelationships, emphasizing the flows of people and of human creations across the earth's surface. The integrating, or synthesizing, theme seeks to bring these two together, emphasizing the totality of interrelationships that makes up a particular location. (The size, or scale, of the location influences the nature of that totality. At some scales certain relationships are vertical, whereas at others they are horizontal; what is intra-regional trade – a vertical relationship – at one scale may be inter-regional trade – a horizontal relationship – at another.)

The history of geography as an academic discipline is such that in many places there is a long and continuing tradition of combining the study of physical and of human geography. Each may be treated separately under both vertical and horizontal themes, but some geographers claim that the integrity of the discipline can only be maintained by seeking to integrate the two. The strength of this tradition is greater in some countries – notably the United Kingdom and its former colonies – than in others; in Sweden and the Netherlands, for example, the two are almost totally divorced. Other countries lie between these two positions; in the United States of America, in particular, the links have been relatively weak in the past, but there is movement towards greater integration at present. The position taken in this book favours the separatist viewpoint, arguing that although by being bracketed together physical and human geographers have undoubtedly learned from each other, basically they operate separately, with human geography increasingly allying itself with the social sciences. It has been argued that certain topics within geography – notably resource analysis and management – integrate human and physical geography, but examination of this claim suggests that it is invalid (Johnston, 1982d).

Human geography is presented here as a social science, therefore, one which studies particular aspects of society relating to space and place. No attempt is made to justify this definition, or to discuss the interrelationships among the social sciences and their debate over the academic division of labour (or even whether such should exist). Human geography exists. The focus here is on what it does, and how it does it. Thus the main concern is with the philosophy of the social sciences and its interpretation for and by human geographers.

Elements of a philosophy of human geography

Any practitioner of an academic discipline undertakes research within a framework provided by a philosophy of that discipline. Such a philosophy may be explicit, in that the researcher has established certain guidelines prior to commencing work, or it may be implicit – there are guidelines but these are not overtly recognized; instead they form part of the researcher's taken-for-granted, everyday world. In the case of an explicit philosophy, this is almost certainly shared with other researchers. With implicit philosophies, however, a greater degree of idiosyncracy is possible, especially in the social sciences.

Philosophy – derived from the Greek and meaning 'love of wisdom' – is a term which is not readily defined, even by philosophers. It is a reflective discipline, involving the consideration of methods of reasoning and argument. The philosophy of a discipline, or group of disciplines, involves the study of the ways in which work is conducted within the disciplinary boundaries (that are, as indicated above, usually defined by subject-matter). The central element in such a philosophy is its *epistemology* or its theory of knowledge; it provides answers to fundamental questions such as 'What can we know?' and 'How can we know it?'. Four aspects of knowledge are covered by epistemology: its nature – what it is that one believes; its type – such as knowledge by acquaintance and knowledge by description (i.e. firsthand and secondhand knowledge); its objects – the facts that are the subject matter of knowledge; and its origins. Associated with epistemology in the philosophical framework is *ontology*, which is the theory of existence or of what can be known. In metaphysics – which is argument about the nature of the world that goes beyond factual issues – the theory of ontology defines what can exist (as, for example, in religions). In the philosophy of academic disciplines, however, it relates to what are accepted as 'facts'.

Every disciplinary philosophy, therefore, contains both an epistemology and an ontology – a framework which defines what we can know and how we can come to know about it. Together these are used to define a *methodology*, a set of rules and procedures which indicates how research and argument are to be conducted within the discipline: how information can be collected and organized. Use of the methodology allows the accumulation of a disciplinary store of knowledge, the results of work aimed at comprehending a particular topic and which are accepted as valid because they were collected within the criteria of epistemology and ontology that are part of the relevant philosophy.

A number of philosophies has been suggested over the centuries. Many are little more than variations on others, and so can be grouped together into categories. For human geography, four such categories are relevant:

1 Empiricist approaches whose epistemology is that we know through experience and whose ontology is that the things we experience are the things that exist – the methodology simply requires a presentation of the experienced facts.

2 Positivist approaches whose epistemology is also that knowledge is gained through experience, but which requires that this experience be firmly established as verifiable evidence on which all will agree. Its ontology is thus one of agreed evidence and its methodology is one of verifying factual statements by what is often known as 'scientific method'.

3 Humanistic approaches whose epistemology is that knowledge is obtained subjectively in a world of meanings created by individuals and whose ontology is that what exists is that which people perceive to exist. Its methodology involves the investigation of these individual worlds and, in opposition to the positivist approaches, emphasizes individuality and subjectivity rather than replicability and truth.

4 Structuralist approaches whose epistemology is that the world of appearances (that which is apprehended) does not necessarily reveal the world of mechanisms (that which causes the world of appearances). To investigate the latter it is necessary to have an ontology which states that what really exists (i.e. the forces creating the world, or the structures) cannot be observed directly but only through thought, and its methodology involves the construction of theories which can account for what is observed but which cannot be tested for their veracity because direct evidence of their existence is not available.

Of these four, the last three cover most of the work being undertaken by human geographers at the present time. As outlined elsewhere (Johnston, 1983a), empiricist approaches declined rapidly in the face of a vigorous campaign for positivist alternatives in the 1950s and 1960s, with the latter decade being characterized by positivist dominance. (Although much work in the positivist genre is very close to being empiricist.) Since then, the humanistic and structuralist approaches have been introduced, initially very much as parts of critiques of positivist work but increasingly as separate schools of human geography making distinctive contributions to a pluralist discipline. The empiricist tradition receives no detailed coverage here, however, because empiricism implies theory and shares many of the ontological and epistemological characteristics of positivism with regard to evidence. (Regional geography, for example, is empiricist, but its usual presentation of material – physical environment before human occupance – implies a theory of environmental influence if not determinism. It does not put its theory to a rigorous test, however.) The other three approaches merit separate chapters. First, however, a brief outline of the development of the discipline is necessary.

The development of human geography

Most disciplines have originated with empiricist practices, not surprisingly since disciplines are defined by what they study and most focus on particular topics which relate to empirical facts. Human geography was no exception to this, and much of its development in the late nineteenth and early twentieth centuries was based on its collection and organization of material about places, which was deemed extremely useful, especially in the growth of the capitalist world economy and the colonial expansion of the period. Not surprisingly, geography developed rapidly in the service of the major colonial powers which required information for mercantile activity. It was strongly linked with expeditions for the gathering of new material, and with the encyclopaedic presentation of such material – in some cases in volumes known as commercial geographies. Associated with this collection of facts was the campaign to propagate them through the educational system, in a school and university discipline designed to widen the horizons and extend the factual knowledge of the average citizen (Freeman 1961, 1980).

Initially, therefore, much of human geography (as part of a general discipline rather than in a full sense separate from physical geography) was concerned with filling in the detail on empty maps and, indeed, in the drawing of the maps themselves. It was strictly empiricist, collecting information and presenting it as fact: its particular methodology involved the cartographic presentation of material.

Out of this collection of facts, relating to both the physical environment and to man's activities on the earth's surface, sprang two separate schools within the discipline. The first – known widely as *environmental determinism* – involved the correlation (in a very general, always verbal, method) of the two sets of information in order to show that the one (the natural environment) was the cause of the other (the spatial distribution and nature of man's activities): places vary in their natural conditions and these variations determine what man does there. This philosophy had an epistemology akin to the positivist, but it had no firm criteria for verifying its statements and no explicit methodology: it was speculation without scientific assessment of its hypotheses and was rapidly discredited.

The other approach – that of *regionalism* – sprang also from contemplation of the material collected in the empiricist tradition, and was to some extent also a reaction to the excesses of environmental determinism. Map comparison showed that certain distributions of phenomena overlapped, creating areas of the earth's surface – regions – with particular combinations of characteristics and producing a unique identity for each area. To some, most notably the French geographers inspired by the work of Paul Vidal de la Blache, each area had its own personality, which could be experienced and identified in the field. The methodology involved the collection of field and other data and its presentation – in cartographic form – to show the unique personality and characteristics of each area. The task of the geographer was to identify the separate areas – the regions – and to define their boundaries. This, too, was essentially an empiricist approach, with the collected facts providing the evidence of differences between places – a theme which became widely known as areal differentiation (Hartshorne, 1939). As practised, much work in this regionalism framework had a strong vein of environmental determinism running through it. Almost invariably, regional geographers presented facts about the physical environment first, and of human activity second, implying a strong causal link between the two. To some, the region could be compared with an organism – something in which the whole is greater than the sum of its parts – and the organic analogy was also used in systematic studies, such as Ratzel's political geography (see Stoddart, 1966).

Development of the regionalism approach required more and more information, and to provide this geography was divided into two main approaches: systematic and regional. The former involved the investigation of particular topics only: it was divided into physical and human, with each being subdivided (the former into geomorphology, climatology, biogeography etc., and the latter into economic geography, social geography etc.). Such specialized systematic approaches were considered necessary for the collation of relevant information, and most geographers were expected to concentrate on one such specialism. But systematic studies were to be subsidiary to regional geography, to the synthesis of material from all specialisms into a regional 'whole', and as well as being a topical specialist each geographer was expected to develop expertise about a particular part of the world.

According to this view of geography, which prevailed into the 1950s, systematic studies were subservient to regional synthesis, thus maintaining the goal of integration as the central point of geography's integrity. To this end, geographers were not encouraged to develop their systematic investigations to such an extent that the regionalism goal was lost sight of. In the United States of America, for example, the study of geomorphology was discouraged, as being properly a part of geology, and only study of 'the geography of landforms' was considered necessary as an input to regional geography.

Despite these constraints suggested by the leaders of the discipline, the study of systematic topics increased in relative importance and was more and more considered a worthwhile end in itself. Regional geography was correspondingly discredited (Freeman, 1980; Gould, 1979).

The expansion of systematic studies led unsurprisingly to closer contacts between geographers and scholars in related disciplines. The geographers retained their perspective on space and place, and many continued to work on particular areas only, without aiming towards the regional synthesis. But these contacts led geographers to appreciate the philosophies of other disciplines and many sought to introduce them – or elements of them – to their own subject. It has been in this way that the split between human and physical geography has become more pronounced in recent decades and that the positivist, humanistic, and structuralist approaches (especially the last two) have been introduced to human geography alone.

The subdivisions of human geography

It is not the aim of the present book to trace the introduction, reception and development of particular approaches to human geography nor to examine international differences in these processes (the former is undertaken in Johnston, 1983a, and the latter in Johnston and Claval, 1983). The emphasis on systematic studies – albeit within the context of space and place – and on the horizontal rather than the vertical interrelationships in contemporary human geography are taken for granted. The focus here is on the philosophies that have been proposed for human geographical study and adopted by some researchers. In seeking to show how these philosophies have been used within the discipline, however, it is necessary to provide a brief outline of its substantive interests.

For this purpose, human geography is divided into four main categories into which most pieces of work fit relatively easy. The first two are by far the largest, and are subdivided into several separate subcategories. *Economic geography* covers the production and distribution of goods and services. Its traditional subcategories are industrial geography, agricultural geography, and transport geography, whose titles clearly indicate the substantive topics covered: the spatial distributions of different industries and agricultural practices were to be described and accounted for, for example. *Social geography* refers more to the consumption of goods and services and to the nature of social life apart from the world of work. Its subcategories include cultural geography, a dominantly North American subject dealing with the interrelationships between cultural groups and environments and with the spread of cultural traits, population geography, urban geography, and rural geography (the last is not particularly well developed). *Political geography*, the third division, is also clearly defined by its title. It, and its subdivision electoral geography, have been relatively weak until recent years. Finally, *historical geography* is another division whose title readily identifies the substantive interests of practitioners: they focus on either or both of the economic/social/political geography of past periods and changing geographies over time; much of this work has been at least implicitly influenced by Darwinian ideas regarding evolution (Stoddart, 1966).

Although, as claimed above, most pieces of work can readily be allocated to one of these divisions and subdivisions, there are areas of overlap and indecision. Within urban geography, for example, the study of residential patterns – of who lives where – is clearly social geography, but the study of central places – of shopping centres within urban areas and the pattern of shopping opportunities and their use over a set of urban places – incorporates the perspectives of both economic and social geographers. Most human geographers associate themselves with one of these divisions, however, if not with one of the subdivisions, but the boundaries are relatively porous and there is much interconnection.

As with the larger world of academic disciplines, so within human geography there are attempts to remove the existing subdivisions. Some of these seek closer integration of the various topical research areas, arguing, for example, that economic and social issues cannot be separated from their political and historical contexts. Thus, for example, there have been arguments for a welfare geography (Smith, 1977) and for a greater emphasis on development studies, both of which seek integration of the whole of human geography around a particular focus rather than its subdivision into what are seen as arbitrary categories the existence of which can be a hindrance to understanding. As will be made clear in Chapter 4, the strongest arguments against these divisions are made by adherents to the structuralist approaches, whose case for a holistic human geography is allied to one for a holistic approach to social science.

In summary

Contemporary human geography is characterized by its division into topical categories and subcategories, each of which analyses the space and place interrelationships of particular substantive elements of society, such as agriculture, industry, and housing. These systematic interests overlay the remains of an earlier geographical focus on regional integration, but whereas many geographers confine their research interests to particular areas of the earth's suface, very few now seek to provide comprehensive surveys and analyses of those areas. Human geography is, then, something of a divided discipline although the divisions, because they are concerned with separate topics, are not necessarily in conflict one with another (except for scarce resources to support research and related activity).

The study of human geography has only recently emerged from its empiricist origins, whose epistemology, ontology and methodology were based on the collection, collation, and presentation of 'facts'. In the last few decades, several other philosophies of human geography have been suggested. Three main ones have been identified here. All are practised at the present time, so that human geography is divided not only in terms of the substance of the work carried out but also in terms of the philosophy of the work. The latter division has generated much more conflict than the former. The next three chapters outline the characteristics of these three approaches, presenting introductory discussions of their epistemologies, ontologies and methodologies and indicating how they have contributed to the literature of human geography. The final chapter looks at various attempts to link the three.

2
Positivist approaches

Positivist approaches are involved with the making of empirical generalizations, statements of a law-like character which relate to phenomena that can be empirically recognized. As such, these approaches are basic to what is widely known as the scientific method, and are central to the methodology and philosophy of the natural sciences. Their application in human geography reflects a belief that similar aims are realizable in what is essentially a social science.

The origins of positivism are traced by many to the French nineteenth century social philosopher August Comte (Lacey, 1976, p. 165). He, according to Andreski (1974, p. 9), 'believed in the supremacy of science' as the only method of investigation, although his developments of positivist ideas were sometimes unusual. To him, the study of science led to the understanding of natural laws, and this understanding allowed society, guided by scientists, to modify nature. Thus:

> Our natural means of acting on the bodies surrounding us are extremely feeble, and quite disproportionate to our needs. Every time we produce a big effect upon nature, it is because the knowledge of natural laws has enabled us to introduce modifying elements . . . so as in certain cases to modify in our interest the final result of a complex of causes. In short: science = foresight, foresight = action (Andreski, 1974, p. 44).

And since Comte believed that scientific methods could be applied to the study of social phenomena, this implies that: first, natural laws can be developed in social sciences; second, these natural laws provide the basis for foresight – i.e. the basis for predictions; and third, the realization of these predictions can be modified by manipulating the causal variables, to change the nature of society.

According to Lacey (1976, 1. 165), Comte used positivism 'to convey six features of things: being real, useful, certain, precise, organic, relative'. Gregory (1978, p. 26, following Habermas, 1972) lists only five: '*le réel, la certitude, le précis, l'utile,* and *le relative*' (organic is omitted). According to these features, science is the study of real, empirically observable phenomena and the relationships between phenomena, and certainty means that there is a common method of observation, so that experiments are replicable in that all scientists proceed in the same way. This common method of working – *le précis* – establishes a unity of scientific method, so that individual sciences are identified by *what* they study rather than *how*. *Le relative* indicates that science proceeds step by step, incorporating new, scientifically-obtained knowledge into established theories and thereby extending its understanding of the world. (The organic feature enters here, in that Comte recognized that 'the more phenomena are general, simple and abstract, the less they depend on other phenomena, the more exact will be the knowledge relating to them, and the more complete will be the co-ordination of that knowledge' (Andreski, 1974, p. 59). Finally, the utility feature implies a central role for scientific knowledge in social engineering: knowledge of the natural laws regarding social phenomena enables society to improve its self-regulation.

Comte's works were published in the period 1830–54, and influenced the conduct of social science inquiry from then on. But the major developments of positivist thinking, to which most contemporary work refers, were undertaken by a group of philosophers (most of them with a scientific rather than a social scientific background) working at the University of Vienna in the 1920s and early 1930s (Kraft, 1953; Hanfling, 1981). Their debates and statements are central to what is known as logical positivism (or logical empiricism).

The logical positivists very largely accepted Comte's outline scheme of a positive science. They codified it with regard to current practice and focused most of their attention on how scientific enquiry might be conducted so as to lead to firmly established generalizations. Theirs was very largely a concern with verification and meaning. Thus:

> the verification of an ordinary statement was to consist of two stages, corresponding to the words 'Logical Empiricism'. The statement would be analysed by a logical process into 'elementary' statements, and then would come the crucial contact with experience, as required by empiricism (Hanfling, 1981, p. 77).

Thus any statement – a proposition – is first analysed and rewritten in ways which allow it to be verified. Such testable statements – hypotheses – are then compared with reality, to establish their veracity.

The fundamentals of positivist science and of logical positivism

Logical positivism is a philosophy concerned with the aquisition of knowledge in the form of general statements, obtained by accepted procedures, about observable phenomena; such statements can then be used in the manipulation of the phenomena. This incorporates what is widely known as scientific method or what Keat (1981, p. 17) calls 'the positivist conception of science'. But the philosophy involves much more, for Keat (p. 15ff.) identifies three other 'doctrines, each of which may not unreasonably be termed 'positivist' ' and adherence to which is central to logical positivism. There are:

1 Scientism which is the claim that the positivist method is the only true method of obtaining knowledge, and that non-positivist methods produce meaningless knowledge. Unless one works according to the scientific method what one has to say is irrelevant and of no value, because it is not verified knowledge.
2 Scientific politics which is the argument that positivism provides the method for finding rational solutions to all problems, so that it offers the basis for social engineering.
3 Value-freedom – the doctrine that scientific judgements are objective, with decisions on the veracity of propositions being made on the basis of criteria that are independent of 'particular moral or political commitments' (p. 18).

All three of these involve making claims that 'science' is relevant in all walks of life and forms of enquiry, and they are represented in some geographical uses of positivism. Critiques of positivist approaches (in geography and elsewhere) in part focus on one or more of these three doctrines as well as on the validity of the scientific method or 'positivist conception of science'. The nature of such critiques must be recognized. For the current discussion, however, the focus is upon *the positivist conception of science*, and on whether the philosophy and methodology of the physical sciences can be validly employed in human geography.

The literature on positivism is large, much of it concerned with minutiae that are irrelevant to a general treatment as conceived here. With regard to human geography, four elements of the positivist programme have been isolated (the first refers to logical positivism; the other three to the positivist conception of science): first, the elimination of metaphysics; second, the centrality of the verification principle; third, the aims of positivist science; and fourth, the structure of positivist science. The four are related, as indicated below, but are treated separately.

The elimination of metaphysics Metaphysics (literally 'after physics') has been defined as the study of questions that 'arise out of, but go beyond, factual or scientific questions about the world' (Lacey, 1976, p. 128). A metaphysician, then, may be defined as someone claiming 'knowledge of a reality which transcended the phenomenal world' (Ayer, 1964, p. 33).

The study of metaphysics is the study of people's experiences and beliefs and of the meanings that they give to things; such experiences, beliefs and meanings cannot be subjected to positivist analysis. As stated by Ayer (1964, p. 41):

> a metaphysical sentence [is] . . . a sentence which purports to express a genuine proposition, but does, in fact, express neither a tautology nor an empirical hypothesis.

(A tautology is a statement which is true in itself, because it says the same thing in two or more ways; most mathematical statements are tautologies. A hypothesis is a statement not yet accepted as true, but whose truth or falsity can be established by recourse to evidence.) The positivist conception of science eliminates such metaphysics and is concerned solely with empirical hypotheses having a factual content:

> every empirical hypothesis must be relevant to some actual, or possible, experience, so that a statement which is not relevant to any experience is not an empirical hypothesis, and accordingly has no factual content (Ayer, 1964, p. 41).

The elimination of metaphysics establishes positivist science as the study of the empirically knowable, and argues that all knowledge must be obtained scientifically. This can be extended into scientism, into statements such as:

> as tautologies and empirical hypotheses form the entire class of significant propositions, we are justified in concluding that all metaphysical assertions are nonsensical (Ayer, 1964, p. 41).

(Note that this was Ayer's position when he published the first edition of *Language, Truth and Logic*, in 1936.) But it is not necessary to proceed this far; metaphysics may be eliminated from certain aspects of human existence, but not all (see Hay, 1979). If this were not so, then it would be difficult for many positivist scientists also to be members of a religious sect (see Flew, 1975).

The verification principle Having established that the positivist conception of science is built around empirical hypotheses – propositions with factual content – a central feature of that science must be the testing of hypotheses: the verification principle. All statements within the science must be genuine:

> a sentence is factually significant to any given person, if, and only if, he knows how to verify the proposition which it purports to express – that is, if he knows what observations would lead him, under certain conditions, to accept the proposition as being true, or reject it as being false (Ayer, 1964, p. 35).

A genuine statement, therefore, must be capable of verification (it is correct) or falsification (it is wrong). Only if a statement is verified is it meaningful for scientific study (i.e. it provides useful knowledge).

The question of verification was central to the work of the Vienna school of logical positivists (Hanfling, 1981). To say that an empirical hypothesis is acceptable only if it can be either verified or not falsified would seem to be relatively straightforward, but the problems of verification are many. Can one achieve 'complete verification', for example, with regard to statements referring to an infinite series of events? ('All men are mortal' is commonly used as an example of such a proposition: Hanfling, 1981, p. 61.) In this case, it seems, one can speak only of incomplete verification: the proposition has yet to be falsified. In other cases, complete verification is possible, since the proposition does not imply an infinite number of occurrences. ('Some men are yetis', for example, would require the observation of only two yetis to be verified. Complete verification would depend, of course, on prior agreement on the definitions for both men and yetis.)

Conclusive verifiability may be impossible with certain classes of propositions, therefore. Thus Ayer, in the introduction to the second edition of *Language, Truth and Logic*, distinguished between what he termed weak and strong verification:

> a proposition is said to be verifiable in the strong sense of the term, if and only if its truth could be conclusively established in experience, but that it is verifiable in the weak sense, if it is possible for experience to render it probable (Ayer, 1964, p. 9)

According to this view, much of positivist science is composed of weakly-verified statements, of propositions which appear to be true, but which remain as 'hypotheses which are continually subject to the test of further experience' (Ayer, 1964, p. 9). Thus while one can identify propositions that can 'be verified conclusively' (p. 10), such *basic propositions* are invariably related 'to the content of a single experience'. However:

> the vast majority of the propositions that people actually express are neither themselves basic statements, nor deducible from any finite set of basic statements (Ayer, 1964, p. 11).

Although one might be certain in one's explanation of a particular event (rainfall at place x being caused by the passage of a cyclone overhead), therefore, one might not be able to reach a strongly-verified conclusion with regard to all such examples of the proposition (that the overhead passage of a cyclone at place x always produces rainfall). With regard to the latter, the positivist scientist has a weakly-verified proposition expressed in terms of probabilities: the likelihood of the outcome. His aim is to strengthen the verification, by increasing the number of verified propositions with regard to the behaviour of the phenomena under consideration.

Thus the positivist conception of science involves the development of verified statements. It is realized, however, that complete verification may not be possible and that strong verification is not always immediately possible, because of the limits of empirical knowledge (Ayer admits also that 'most empirical propositions are in some degree vague' p. 12). Thus science is cumulative. Hay (1979, p. 9) expresses it in slightly different terms:

> the question to be asked of a geographic theory is not 'does this theory *totally* explain the observed variation?' but the more modest question, 'does this theory contribute an explanation of a part of the observed variation which would otherwise remain obscure?'

(In the terms of the present discussion, for 'theory' substitute 'proposition' or 'empirical hypothesis'.)

Positivist science proceeds by the verification of propositions, according to the common view. However, one philosopher associated with, though never a member of, the Vienna school has argued against the use of the verification principle as the central focus of positivist methodology and has replaced it by the falsification principle. Popper had observed that a theory, or series of propositions, could continue to be accepted if some evidence favoured it:

> no theory could ever be relied on to be the final truth. The most we can ever say is that it is supported by every observation so far, and yields more, and more precise, predictions than any known alternative. It is still replaceable by a better theory (Magee, 1973, p. 29).

But why and how to produce that better theory, if the existing one is being verified? Popper's solution rests in the problem of complete verification: although a proposition may not be conclusively verifiable it can be (indeed must be) conclusively falsifiable. In this way, Popper claims one can separate science from pseudo-science by the following:

> If somebody proposed a scientific theory he should answer, as Einstein did, the question: 'Under what conditions would I admit that my theory is untenable?'. In other words, what conceivable facts would I accept as refutations, or falsifications, of my theory? (Popper, 1976, p. 41).

Falsification would add to knowledge, since it showed where the theory (proposition) failed, a piece of information more valuable than another piece of verification because it indicates the lacunae in knowledge and the areas for further work. Thus Popper's scientific method (sometimes termed critical rationalism) proceeds by the conduct of critical experiments designed to refute propositions: if a proposition is not falsified, the experiment has corroborated it, but not confirmed its validity.

The aims of positivist science Whether one proceeds by the verification or the falsification route, positivist science according to this discussion seeks to establish the veracity of propositions (empirical hypotheses) about the phenomena under discussion. As indicated in the outline of the verification principle, this veracity may be established with regard to particular circumstances, and produce a basic proposition, or it may be phrased more widely, producing a general proposition whose application is not specific to a particular set of circumstances. The aim of positivist science is to achieve the latter, which will encapsulate the former; if we can provide general explanations, then clearly we can explain particular realizations of the phenomena under investigation.

This aim is usually expressed as the search for scientific laws. Thus:

> The function of a science . . . is to establish general laws covering the behaviour of the empirical events or objects with which the science in question is concerned, and thereby to enable us to connect together our knowledge of the separately known events, and to make reliable predictions of events as yet unknown (Braithwaite, 1953, p. 1).

A law, according to Braithwaite (1953, p. 12), is:

> equivalent to [a] generalization of unrestricted range in space and time of greater or lesser degrees of complexity of generality.

It is a statement whose only qualification concerns the subject matter to which it relates and 'the fundamental aim of a science is the establishment of such laws' (p. 2). With them, it is then possible to tackle the explanation of particular events (although, of course, it may well be the existence of such events that stimulates the search for a law: see below). The methodology for achieving the aim of producing laws is the subject of a later section of this chapter (pp. 18-25).

The structure of positivist science Positivist science, according to this outline, is a means of attaining objective knowledge about the world, knowledge which is independent of the scientists. To achieve this, science must not only have certain aims, as described above, but also agreed procedures. Thus Mulkay (1975) suggests that scientists must conform to the following norms:

1 Originality – their aim is to advance knowledge, by the discovery of new material.
2 Communality – all knowledge is shared, with its provenance fully recognized.
3 Disinterestedness – scientists are interested in knowledge for its own sake, and their only reward is the satisfaction that they have advanced understanding.
4 Universalism – judgements are on academic grounds only, and incorporate no reflections on the individuals concerned.
5 Organized scepticism – knowledge is advanced by constructive criticism.

If these norms are met, science is conducted in a neutral fashion, without partiality, self-seeking, secrecy or intellectual prejudice; objective criteria are applied in all assessments, and scientists are humble individuals.

Positivist approaches

This leads to what Mulkay (1979, pp. 19–20) calls the 'standard view of science':

> the natural world is to be regarded as real and objective. Its characteristics cannot be determined by the preferences or intentions of its observers. These characteristics can, however, be more or less faithfully represented. Science is that intellectual enterprise concerned with providing an accurate account of the objects, processes and relationships occurring in the world of natural phenomena. . . . Although the natural world is, in a certain sense, undergoing continuous change and movement, there exist underlying and unchanging uniformities. These basic empirical regularities can be expressed as universal and permanent laws of nature, which tell us what is always and everywhere the case. Unbiased, detached observation furnishes the evidence on which these laws are built.

Science is conducted within this framework. Further, the concept of a social science that can be subject to the same positivist method, and which according to some includes human geography, implies the belief that all that has been outlined here applies to the so-called 'human world' as well as to the 'natural world'. The remainder of this chapter is concerned with the working-out of that contention and the search for 'universal and permanent laws' in the social science of human geography. (This, of course, avoids the contention by some that human geography is not a social science.)

At this point, the differences between positivism, as it will be used here, and logical positivism should be stressed. Positivism is what Keat calls the positivist conception of science, or what is frequently termed scientific method: it involves rigorous enquiry and the search for generalizations. It is a part of, but only a part of, logical positivism. This latter not only advances a particular mode of inquiry – the scientific method – but also claims that this is the sole valid route to knowledge. Anything else is metaphysical, and thus non-scientific (and nonsense). Thus logical positivism embraces scientism, scientific politics, and value-freedom as well as the positivist conception of science. It is an ideology as well as a philosophy and methodology. Whereas positivism is the search for generalizations via a rigorous procedure, logical positivism is the argument that this is the only path to knowledge.

The methodology of positivism

Positivist science is built on the verification principle. To know that something is true is to know, and to accept, the method of substantiating its truth. (If someone says something is true, that statement is accepted because the method by which it was reached – i.e. how the proposition was verified – is accepted.) Thus verification implies a methodology. This is indicated in a passage (quoting Waismann) by Hanfling (1981, p. 24) which indicates the link between methodology and epistemology:

> To understand a proposition means to know what is the case if the proposition is true. One can understand it without knowing *whether* it is true.
>
> To become aware of the sense of a proposition one has to get clear about the procedure for establishing its truth. If one does not know this procedure, then one cannot understand the proposition either.
>
> *The sense of a proposition is the method of its verification.* (His italics)

One accepts that a statement is true only because one accepts that the method of establishing its veracity is valid. Thus the positivist conception of science must incorporate an accepted methodology.

This methodology goes under a large variety of titles including, simply, 'the scientific method' and also the hypothetico-deductive method. Its aim, as outlined above, is the production of laws, but not simply laws as isolated statements. To be truly meaningful in a scientific sense, laws should be embedded within a theory, which sets them in context, links them with other laws, and provides a unity for the particular science. Thus the aim of producing laws is part of a more general aim, that of producing theories.

A scientific theory, according to the positivist view, comprises a particular deductive system, which is composed of two elements: a set of initial propositions (or assumptions) and a set of deduced, or empirical, propositions (hypotheses) which follow from them, because of the operation of the laws (themselves part of the initial propositions) within the system. The development of the theory involves the deduction of new propositions. The logical sequence from assumption to deduced proposition, to another deduced proposition, and so on, through a continuous chain is likened by most philosophers of science to a calculus (Braithwaite, 1953).

In an abstract science, such as mathematics, the deduced propositions of the scientific theory are not given any external meaning. The theory is self-contained, and any hypotheses derived can be verified within it because of the tautologous characteristic of mathematics. This is not so with empirical sciences, however, in which the hypotheses relate to some (pre-defined) phenomena. In order for the theory to be extended, by the incorporation of the deduced propositions into the initial propositions, the validity of the deduced propositions must be verified by an accepted methodology. This is the methodology of hypothesis-testing.

A hypothesis is an empirical proposition, a statement of what should be, given certain conditions; it is deduced from what is already known (or assumed) and is an attempted *explanation*. If it is true, then it is a scientific law, within the prescribed domain of that law (i.e. the range of phenomena, conditions etc. to which it applies), which *explains* the phenomenon under investigation. Thus:

> a scientific hypothesis is a general proposition about all the things of a certain

sort. It is an empirical proposition in the sense that it is testable by experience; experience is relevant to the question as to whether or not the hypothesis is true, i.e. as to whether or not it is a scientific law (Braithwaite, 1953, p. 2).

This raises two main issues for an empirical science: the derivation of hypotheses, and the testing procedure.

The derivation of hypotheses
In an abstract science such as mathematics, hypotheses are derived by processes of logical reasoning from a priori assumptions, which should be accepted laws. Such logical reasoning will be of the form 'Given x, then y follows', and the veracity of y can be established through accepted mathematical procedures of reasoning. (It results in the acronym QED – *quod erat demonstrandum*.) In an empirical science, the process is that a set of givens (the known laws) is taken. From them a potential new law is deduced, and presented as a hypothesis. The veracity of this hypothesis can then be tested by experiment (or confounded by a critical experiment designed to falsify it).

But what of an empirical science with few established laws, especially if the laws are irrelevant to the particular subject matter being considered? In this case, the deductive procedure is likely to be relatively barren, and to produce few testable empirical hypotheses. Instead, the scientist is forced to speculate on less certain ground, to produce hypotheses with less substantial bases, perhaps using analogies or metaphors to advance his potential understanding of a particular topic (Harrison and Livingstone, 1982).

Two major sources for the empirical scientist in this situation are personal experiences (plus, perhaps, the reports of those of others) and a reading of the results of other scientific experiments. With regard to the former, sense experiences are perhaps the major stimulus to work in certain sciences. The scientist observes certain phenomena, either in the course of his work or in his everyday life. He is led (by his natural curiosity if nothing else) to speculate about these phenomena. He is seeking laws to account for their existence, and he may accumulate evidence to back up his speculations.

This process of law-making by the accumulation of evidence is criticized by positivist scientists. Rather than proceeding from the general to the specific – from the proposition to the test – and thence, if valid, back to the general (the law), it proceeds from the specific to the general without any intervening critical test. This is the problem of *induction* (or inductive reasoning), in which the premisses are presented as logical consequences of their conclusion, rather than the other way round (Braithwaite, 1953, p. 258). Induction, according to Lacey (1976, p. 94), is:

> any rational process where from premises about some things of a certain kind a conclusion is drawn about some or all of the remaining things of that kind.

This is invalid as a form of reasoning, because the 'sample' of things actually observed may be very biased (as Lacey puts it, 'the smaller n is, the weaker the argument will be', p. 94), and because the observation that certain consequences are associated with certain antecedent conditions cannot incorporate situations where such conditions are not associated with those consequences.

Induction can be the source of hypotheses, therefore, but not of generalizations and laws. (Because of the problem of incomplete verification, however – see p. 16 – much positivist science includes an inductive component. Because the populations of many phenomena are finitely large, if not infinite, verification of hypotheses is conducted on samples only, which may be biased. The generalizations drawn are correspondingly weak.) For generalizations to be made, the hypothesis must be properly tested according to accepted procedures. There is no doubt, however, that induction can be extremely stimulating to scientific advance, especially if it involves the scientist placing observations in the context of accepted theories.

All work, therefore, in empirical sciences begins with images of the world. These images may be derived entirely from existing theory, or they may be derived from some combination of (relatively unstructured, i.e. not in the context of the test of a hypothesis) empirical observation, consideration of the findings of other sciences, and accepted theory. From them, if the scientist is to develop laws and extend the available theory, hypotheses must be deduced and stated as testable propositions.

A commonly-used device for the development of hypotheses is the *model*, which provides a formal structuring of the images. The term model has been used in a variety of ways by scientists (not least by geographers: Chorley and Haggett, 1967, Chapter 1). In the sense implied here, however, it is a representation of a segment of the world, as the scientist believes it to be structured. This representation involves not a series of relatively unordered observations but a formal 'picture', one from which a hypothesis may be derived. It is thus an aid to hypothesis-derivation. It may be a formal ordering of observations, or it may be a representation of part of a theory. Whatever its provenance, its purpose is to further the presentation and testing of hypotheses.

Hypothesis-testing
Perhaps the most critical stage in the methodology of positivist science is the testing of hypotheses. In this, the propositions are to be set against empirical data.

Empirical hypotheses may take a number of forms, including:

1 If A, then B – if event A occurs, then event B will follow.
2 $B = f(A)$ – the magnitude of event B, at a place, is a function of the magnitude of event A there.

3 If no A, then no B – if event A does not occur, then event B will not occur.

4 If A, then no B – if event A occurs, then event B will not occur.

These can clearly be tested against empirical evidence. With regard to hypothesis 1, for example, occurrences of event A could be investigated to see whether event B followed; if not, the hypothesis is falsified. The procedure seems very straightforward, but two major problems arise.

The first problem relates to the issue of complete verification discussed earlier. If the context of the hypothesis is not finite then it can never be firmly established if it is valid, only whether it is confirmed by available data. This problem of the (potential) infinity of tests relates to the universal content of (many) hypotheses, though not exclusively so. It has been extended in much work to the related problem not of the infinite number of potential tests but to the very large number. Should every possible test be conducted, or is it possible to make a generalization regarding the veracity of the hypothesis from a sample of tests, and how should that sample be selected?

The answer to this second problem has been sought in the development of the (abstract) science of statistics, particularly that branch known as inferential statistics which is based on probability theory. The basis of this theory is that it allows statements to be made of the form 'given that I have an unbiased sample of x observations, taken from a known population y, I can conclude that the result I have observed relating to that sample also holds for the population from which the sample was drawn, at a given level of probability' (i.e. I can express my degree of certainty about this statement, ranging from 0.0 – complete uncertainty – to 1.0 – complete certainty). To be able to make such a statement implies that I know the population from which the sample has been drawn, and that the sample has been taken in such a way that no member of the population has a greater or lesser chance of being studied than does any other.

There is also a problem relating to the use of the verification principle rather than that of falsification. It asks 'how well do the empirical data have to fit in order for me to accept the hypothesis as valid?'. (For the falsification principle, the answer would be 'perfectly'; one failure and the hypothesis would be confounded. Using sample data, however, this would not avoid the problem of how one could be sure that there were no confounding tests in the population at large.) Thus with regard to hypothesis 4 above, what proportion of events in which both B and A occurred would lead me to decide that the hypothesis is invalid?

The solution to this problem is again usually found in probability theory. To return to hypothesis 4, it may be that 20 occurrences have been studied: in 10, event A has been observed but not event B; in 8, event B has been observed but not event A; and in 2, both events A and B have been observed. Probability theory is then asked, 'Given that 12 occurrences of event A take place, and 10 of event B, what is the likelihood that as few as 2 of those events will occur simultaneously?'. In other words, in a population with a similar proportion of events A and B, what is the likelihood that the two events will occur together by chance? The smaller this probability, the more certain the scientist is that his hypothesis is valid; the confounding cases occur very rarely (in relative terms) and can be associated either with chance (some random process that is not identified in his hypothesis) or with another mechanism not identified as yet in his theory/model. In terms of the quotation from Hay (see above, p. 16), the test has provided evidence that the hypothesis – and the model from which it is drawn – is contributing to the development of an explanation of the subject-matter.

Hypothesis-testing, then, involves the collection of empirical evidence with which to assess the veracity of the hypothesis. Because hypotheses, as preludes to scientific laws, are assumed to have universal properties across a pre-defined empirical domain, conclusive tests are often impossible, and in many cases all possible events cannot be studied. Thus the scientists must devise tests (experiments, collection of data) according to strictly-defined procedures regarding populations and samples, so that it is possible to make statements regarding the former from the latter. Further, in many empirical sciences the investigator accepts that all speculations are incomplete and cannot incorporate every eventuality. It may be, therefore, that hypothesis 4 should be 'If A and C, then no B', but the theory and model did not include C. Thus the scientist is interested in the likelihood that the existence of A means that B will not be present. If his conclusion is only a likelihood, he may conclude that A is a necessary but an insufficient condition for the non-existence of B; study of the deviant cases may lead him to formulate the new hypothesis 'If A and C, then no B', which must be tested in a new experiment, independent of the previous one, otherwise he faces the problem of induction. (Note that 'If A and C, no B' is not symmetrical with 'If no B, then A and C'. This is a separate hypothesis, implying a different theory.)

Included in this discussion of hypothesis-testing are the notions of randomness and chance events. In a complete scientific explanation, these should not occur, unless there are elements of the phenomena being studied whose behaviour is entirely random. A belief that this is so is contrary to a basic assumption of positivist science that everything can be explained, that all events have a determinate cause. Randomness may be allowed to enter, however, if:

1 The study is being conducted at an aggregate level, of how a mass of individuals behaves rather than each individual, in which case the

aggregation process may involve averaging, around which the individual variation can be treated as random.

2 The study is only partial in that its hypotheses specify only part of the relationship (i.e. 'If A and C then B' is the complete hypothesis but only 'If A then B' is being studied) and it can be assumed that the effect of the other variables is the same as random.

3 If measurement error, which is unbiased and therefore random, has taken place. (This last assumes that the elements in the hypothesis being tested – A, B and C or whatever – can be both isolated and measured in the 'real world'.)

In such situations, the investigator may be prepared to accept some randomness in the relationship being studied, and asks whether the result that has been observed is very likely to have occurred simply by the random allocation of the observations. If probability theory indicates that the likelihood of a random occurrence of such a relationship is very small, the analyst concludes that the result obtained is 'real' and indicative of the operation of the law he is seeking to establish.

Theories, models, hypotheses, and laws

Science is a cumulative process, therefore, whereby knowledge is acquired in a structured manner so that every additional piece contributes to scientists' comprehension of the world. It begins with theories, and ends with them. The aim is to extend existing theories, by incorporating within them the findings from the latest round of speculation, the newly-established laws.

As a science develops, so does its body of theory(ies). Initially, it will be in a state of weak theoretical development, probably lacking any established laws. The first rounds of model-building and hypothesis-generation will not be atheoretical, however, since this implies that the process of thinking takes place in some sort of vacuum. All thought is theoretically guided, although often by a weak, if not inaccurate, theory. (It is for this reason that pure empiricism is impossible. Any work, however unstructured, is guided by notions of what is worth thinking about. In human geography, any data collection is influenced by theories of what is worth measuring – and mapping.) Scientists are socialized into the processes of scientific research and into the substance of disciplines, and the bodies of knowledge and research methodologies that they learn structure the ways in which they identify and tackle new problems (see Kuhn, 1962; Barnes, 1982). When faced with a new situation, they will react to it in the context of what they already know, seeking to incorporate it within their existing theoretical framework and to develop laws about it using their established methodology. Thus positivist science is a conservative process, with knowledge accumulating along predetermined lines (allowing some scope, of course, for the individual whims of the scientists; however, scientists are considerably constrained in that, in many cases, certain problems must remain insoluble until others have been solved). Occasionally, it is necessary to break this conservatism, to bring fresh light onto problems, not by starting *de novo* but by tackling the problems in the context of a different theoretical structure, a different set of initial propositions leading to new deductions which may demand development of a new methodology, before they can be tested.

Each scientist, then, is presented in his education with a method of thinking about research problems – a theoretical structure – and a procedure for testing hypotheses – a research methodology. His tasks involve using the theoretical structure plus his observations of the world (including, perhaps, the results from work in other theoretical structures) to identify as-yet unsolved research problems. This may involve the derivation of a new model or the creation of a new concept, but in many cases problems will be identified within existing models. Hypotheses are generated; experiments are designed to test them; data are gathered; and the test is concluded. The result (hopefully) is positive, and a further law – a scientific generalization – is added to the theoretical structure.

Most scientists are involved in all aspects of this procedure to a greater or lesser extent. Some are happier to work in the theoretical structure, to manipulate the known information in the search for new questions. Others may prefer to work at the modelling stage, representing ideas in a formal manner. And still others may prefer to be experimenters, collecting data and testing hypotheses generated by others. Such a division of labour is for convenience only. Science is a continuous, integrated process of structuring, speculating, and experimenting.

Not all scientific effort is successful. If it fails – the hypothesis is not verified, or the critical experiment leads to a falsification of the hypothesis – this could be for one or more of several reasons. The failure may have been in the structuring: the theory and the model were wrongly assembled. Or the speculations were in error: the hypothesis was applied to irrelevant situations, perhaps indicating that existing theory applies to a more restricted empirical domain than was originally believed. Or the testing was invalid: the experiment was improperly conducted perhaps. Such negative findings are valuable in pointing future work in more fruitful directions – the failures usually indicate the fallibility of scientists rather than the fallibility of science!

Positivist social science

The above description of positivist science outlines the basis of a unified structure which is applicable, according to Comte and the many who have followed him, to the social sciences as much as to the natural sciences. As a structure it has been developed almost entirely by and for natural scientists, however, and has only been adapted for the social sciences. As such, the application of positivism in the social sciences (i.e. to the study of individuals and society) is based on the premise of *naturalism*, the 'doctrine that there can be a natural scientific study of society' (Thomas, 1979). This in turn is founded on certain assumptions, which can be enumerated as follow:

1 That events which occur within a society, or which involve human decision-making, have a determinate cause, that is identifiable and verifiable. This is the assumption of *causation* (i.e. that A, B, and C in the hypothesis – p. 19 – can be isolated and linked in a particular way).

2 That decision-making is the result of the operation of a set of laws, to which individuals conform. This can be called the assumption of *behaviourism*, that a given stimulus produces a particular response under predefined circumstances.

3 That there is an objective world, comprising individual behaviour and the results of that behaviour, which can be observed and recorded in an objective manner, on universally-agreed criteria. This is the assumption of (direct or naïve) *realism*. Without it, use of the positivist procedure would be impossible since this is based on the acceptance of evidence, 'the sense of a proposition is the method of its verification', and so, if the nature of the evidence is not acceptable to all, the application of the procedures is impossible. (Note that this form of realism differs from transcendental realism, discussed in Chapter 4.)

4 That the scientist is a disinterested observer, able to stand outside his subject matter (even though in another segment of his life he may be a part of it). He can observe and record its features in a neutral way, without in any aspect changing those features by his procedures, and can reach dispassionate conclusions about it, which can be verified by other observers. This is the assumption of the *disinterested observer*.

5 That, as in the study of inanimate matter, there is a structure to human society (an organic whole) which changes in determinate ways, according to the observable laws. This can be called the *functionalism* assumption, that the various elements in society occupy a particular location within it.

6 That the application of the laws and theories of positivist social science can be used to alter societies, again in determinate ways, either by changing the laws which operate in particular circumstances or by changing the circumstances in which the laws will operate. This can be called the *social engineering* assumption.

The existence of these assumptions, whose underpinning of all positivist social science may go unrecognized by many practitioners, does not imply a crude, mechanistic model of society involving simple laws of cause and effect (if A, then B), although many such have been proposed. Human societies are complex, perhaps more complex than the subject matter of natural sciences, but complexity should not, according to Thomas (1979), be presented as a reason for not seeking to unravel society. It means that there are many rather than few laws operating, a large proportion under very restricted circumstances, but interacting with many others. This leads some to argue that each event, each item of human decision-making, is unique. The response to this is that its uniqueness represents a unique combination of circumstances, and thus operation of the relevant laws, rather than a singular situation which is incomparable with any other. Thus:

> Wide differences in the manifest characteristics and behaviour of a group of phenomena do not exclude there being a common set of variables that underlie and can be used to explain all the phenomena; to think otherwise is to make the cardinal confusion of generalisations with initial conditions (Thomas, 1979, p. 18).

Because the laws are likely to be many, and the circumstances in which they operate very much more numerous in type, the process of uncovering the laws is likely to be slow. Comprehension is extended with each round of successful research, providing an empirical generalization which, while lacking the universality required of a law, furthers knowledge of the phenomena being studied.

The argument, therefore, is that the positivist model of science can be applied within social science. It is built on the assumptions outlined above, which can be reduced to one sentence: human behaviour is subject to the operation of laws of cause and effect, and the nature of these laws can be identified by the process of hypothesis-testing against empirical evidence. By looking at society in a particular way, it will tell us how it works. Note that some would argue that the laws are never deterministic – they never provide complete verification – because man has 'free will'. There are two basic responses to this. The first is to claim that man's freedom to choose is limited and that all behaviour and beliefs are ultimately determined; the problem is the inability of social science to identify the causal chains. This is the logical positivist argument associated with the elimination of metaphysics. (The failure may be accommodated in the short-run – until the development of better theories – by the incorporation of random error in the preferred explanation to encompass what is presented as free will but is, in fact, as-yet unexplained variation.) The second response is to accept that the positivist conception of science does not apply to all aspects of social science. In this case, the assumptions listed above are qualified in the single sentence statement so that: some aspects of human behaviour are subject to the operation of laws of cause and effect and can be studied according to the positivist conception of science. Others cannot, so that positivism relates to a limited domain. In logical positivism, as applied to the social sciences, there is no such limitation.

Positivism and human geography

Human geography was one of the last of the social sciences to adopt positivist approaches on a wide scale. In part this was because of its relatively weak links with the other social sciences until relatively recently; in part because its main links to the natural sciences, through physical geography, were with geology, in which positivism was not dominant (empiricism was, and so were the evolutionary ideas introduced by Darwin and widely adopted in the earth and life sciences, see Stoddart, 1966); and in part because of its firm base in the humanities (alongside a non-social scientific history) and the exceptionalist philosophy, the promotion of the unique codified by Hartshorne (1939). No precise date for the introduction of positivist approaches to the discipline can be identified, for there were elements of them in isolated papers. But it was in the mid- and late-1950s in the United States of America that widespread introduction occurred, at a number of institutions (Johnston, 1983a). From these it spread rapidly, dominating the discipline throughout North America and much of the rest of the English-speaking world by the end of the 1960s.

Reasons for the adoption of positivist approaches were varied and are not readily uncovered. In general, they seem to be related to disgruntlement with existing approaches (see Gould, 1979) and the attractions of a 'scientific' social science, as being practised in economics, sociology, psychology, and politics. (There were also links, via physical geographers, to geologists introducing positivist procedures, such as Krumbein, Schumm and Strahler.) Science was academically and socially respectable, and so was social science; it was useful, and geographers perceived that they, by becoming more scientific, could become useful too, so advancing disciplinary and personal esteem.

Whatever the general attraction of the positivist approaches, it is clear that in most cases these were not fully assimilated into geographical training. There was little evidence of courses in philosophy of science or even in scientific method, nor of any study of these subjects by the proponents of the positivist conception of science. The major terms – law, model, theory, and hypothesis – were all widely used, but the main impression is one of only partial appreciation of the details of the positivist arguments. Some advanced the three other arguments noted by Keat – scientism, scientific politics, and value-freedom – without a great deal of careful analysis (or so it appears in hindsight).

But the bandwagon rolled on. To many, it seemed, the major attraction of the positivist approaches was quantification: the expression of research results in mathematical or statistical form, in a way which implied precision, replicability, and certainty (*la certitude* of Comte). Thus a number of the proponents of the new approaches called themselves 'statistical geographers'.

Indeed, their arguments were widely known as the 'quantitative revolution', as indicated in a widely-referenced paper by Burton (1963), which heralded the success of that revolution and the likely ensuing:

> mathematization of much of our discipline, with an attendant emphasis on the construction and testing of theoretical models (Burton, 1963, p. 151).

Most revolutions are taken to excess by some of the proponents, and there is little doubt that some of the early work was relatively trivial, led by the availability of data, and involving the testing of hypotheses that were weakly linked, at best, to any well-articulated theory or model. (The term hypothesis, for example, was much abused at the time, Newman, 1973.) Nevertheless, to suggest that positivist approaches were being widely misused and abused is to overstate the case. There was considerable debate centred on certain fundamental aspects of the relevance of the positivist conception to geographical work, with reference to the literature of the philosophy of science. Chorley (1964), for example, published a classic paper on the role of models in geographical work, with the term 'model' being defined in a very catholic way, to incorporate theory; this paper was the precursor to a widely-acclaimed large volume on the theme of models in geography (Chorley and Haggett, 1967). The relevance of laws was discussed too, with an important short paper by Lewis (1965, p. 27) concluding that:

> It was agreed that, logically, everything is unique. But similarities can be found among unique things and general statements can be made from these similarities. These statements are then expressed as formal laws. These laws do not imply that one event A is always followed by another event B, but they state a functional relationship between given determinants. Finally, it was seen that determinism in this sense involves no conflict with introspective free will.

Golledge and Amedeo (1968) also tackled the important issue of laws in and for geography, arguing from the premise that 'the ultimate existence of laws is predicated on accepting the principle of rationality or non-randomness in a universe' to the conclusion that 'Presenting research results in a rigorous manner and examining the possibility that a form of lawfulness may have been discovered is as good a way as any to start developing a meaningful and sound philosophical base in the discipline' (p. 774). Finally, several authors (including Grigg, 1965) examined the relationships between the traditional geographical interest in regionalization (the division of the earth's surface into types) and the more general scientific procedure of classification (the identification of individuals with common features and thus subject to the same laws).

A full statement of, and argument for, a positivist approach in human

was not published until 1969. Drawing on the writings of
members of the Vienna school and its followers, Harvey's (1969)
... in Geography emphasized methodological rather than philosophical issues. He accepted the assumptions of the positivist conception of a (social) science and devoted virtually all of his attention to its *modus operandi* in a geographical context. Thus at the outset of the book he argued for the centrality of explanation as the focus of geographical work and for the scientific method as the set of rules which governed the acceptance/non-acceptance of a proposed explanation. He then discussed the issues involved in applying these rules in the social sciences – noting that in their application most 'have not been particularly rigorous' and that 'Each discipline tends to be autonomous with respect to the criteria it employs in deciding whether or not statements are justified' (p. 60–1) – and examined the history of attitudes to theory in geography. He concluded, with Ballabon (1957, p. 218), that geography is 'short on theory and long on facts' and argued that:

> the development of theory appears vital both to satisfactory explanation and to the identification of geography as an independent field of study (p. 78).

This led to his conclusion to the book, that geographers should:

> create theoretical structures which, in turn, will give our discipline the identity and direction it so badly needs at the present time. Without theory we cannot hope for controlled, consistent, and rational, explanation of events. Without theory we can scarcely claim to know our own identity (p. 486).

Given this end, Harvey contended that there is much misunderstanding about the means of a positivist conception of science and about the roles of its central elements: theories, laws, models, and hypotheses. Thus these are given extended treatment, as are the roles of mathematics ('the language of science') and probability ('the language of chance'). What Harvey provided, therefore, was a series of insights into the major elements of the positivist conception of science, set within a framework of belief that the development of a body of theory (scientifically-obtained) is necessary for a scientific discipline to obtain independent status.

It is interesting to note that, although Harvey drew considerably on the writings of the logical positivists, he did not argue for scientism. He noted with regard to temporal studies, for example (pp. 80–81), that one should not impute an historical determinism to unfolding landscapes; and he argued that 'It is not the role of the methodologist ... to curb speculation, to decry metaphysics, to chain the imagination' (p. 481) and that, in the context of the scientist as decision-maker, 'Decisions cannot be made in a moral or ethical vacuum' (p. 40). He presented a methodology. Clearly he believed it to be of considerable and widespread value to geographers, for he continues on p. 481 from the quote above that:

> at some stage we have to pin down our speculations, separate fact from fancy, science from science fiction. It is the task of the methodologist to point to the tools which can be used to accomplish this, to assess their efficiency and worth.

This comes close to arguing for scientism, and it leads on to the already quoted statement that:

> Without theory we cannot hope for controlled, consistent, and rational, explanation of events (p. 486).

But, as he admits in that book and elsewhere (Harvey, 1973), philosophical issues were very largely avoided (neither epistemology nor ontology is in the index). Thus *Explanation in Geography* was basically a presentation of scientific methodology and as such was positivist. Any suggestion of logical positivism was very much implicit.

The content of positivist human geography

Positivists, as indicated earlier, believe in the unity of the scientific method. It is not how their particular research is conducted which distinguishes between disciplines according to this view, therefore, but what they study, since all use the same methodology. Thus the development of a positivist geography required the development of a particular focus, which bestowed upon human geography a separate identity within the social sciences. It was to be the scientific method applied to a particular, geographical, subject matter.

The chosen focus, building on the earlier traditions within the discipline, was 'place and space'. As Harvey (1969, p. 191) expressed it:

> The whole practice and philosophy of geography depends upon the development of a conceptual framework for handling the distribution of objects and events in space.

Geographers had long been interested in 'What is where?', which can be broken down into two related questions: 'What complex of phenomena characterize a particular place?' and 'What distribution pattern characterizes a particular phenomenon?'. The two are clearly linked. What is in a particular place reflects the distributions of various phenomena, whereas those distributions may be influenced by the attractions of particular places (because of what is already present) for certain phenomena.

Within this focus, certain aspects of space were emphasized, notably its role as an impedance factor. To cross space involves time, various costs, and other factors. These costs are to be avoided as far as possible, and so the organization of society is spatially structured to keep down, if not to minimize, the so-called 'frictions of distance'. Thus to many, human

...ame the study of 'spatial science' (or spatial social science), ...s were made to develop theories reflecting this position (e.g. ...963). Alongside this, attempts were made to justify such a ... and focus within the social sciences (e.g. Cox, 1976).

Th.. theme of a spatial focus for human geography evolved out of its previous concerns with the characteristics of places (i.e. regionalism) and was a positivist approach to the topic of areal differentiation. If unique events (in geography, places) result from particular combinations of general laws (in geography, those of spatial distributions), then the characteristics of those events (places) can only be explained by an articulation of the relevant laws. These laws, of course, have status conferred on them in terms of their theoretical location: the theories are located in systematic rather than regional geography, hence the 'downgrading' of the latter. Spatial science required theories, therefore, from which models and hypotheses could be derived and tested. Initially, a few main topics were developed in this way. In each case, the theoretical basis was drawn from outside human geography, mainly other social sciences. In those, they were relatively minor foci, but in geography, they were elevated to a central importance (see Pooler, 1977). (The only competition was from regional science, a new discipline – based in economics – with a similar focus. This has never attracted many member academics, however, and teaches relatively few students because it has failed to establish an institutional base in more than a few universities. In recent decades, only geography has emphasized spatial aspects within the social sciences.)

Central place theory This is a theory (really, a family of theories) of the size, functions, and spatial distributions of settlements which provide services for the populations of hinterlands. Its twin origins lay in the work of two German economist-geographers, Walter Christaller and August Losch, although several other authors had noted some of the empirical regularities whose existence the theories generalized.

Central place theory, in its simplest form, is based on the following initial propositions: that entrepreneurs locate service establishments to maximize turnover, which involves them being as close to their customers as possible; that customers purchase goods and services from the nearest available outlet; that different types of establishment require different levels of turnover, and thus different sizes of customer populations, to support their existence; and that there are no impediments to movement, the costs of which are linearly related to the distance travelled. From these it was deduced that establishments – and thus settlements – should be uniformly distributed in areas of uniform population density, and that the clustering of establishments with similar turnover levels should (according to Christaller's theory but not Losch's) create a hierarchical structure of settlements.

Central place theory is based, therefore, on certain assumed laws of behaviour. From it was developed a model of a settlement pattern. This provided a number of testable hypotheses related to the size, spacing and functional composition of settlements, and also of shopping centres within urban areas. It stimulated a large volume of empirical work. As well as investigations of the deduced regularities, numerous researchers also used the initial propositions as the bases for hypotheses, particularly that with regard to consumers shopping at the nearest available outlet. Few of the studies found the theory provided a full explanation of observed distributions, but most found some conformity between hypothesis and evidence and concluded that the experiment (test) had at least partially verified the theory and the assumptions on which it is based. (See Beavon, 1976.)

Land-use theory This developed a theory of the organization of agricultural land-uses about a market, formalized by a German economist, J. H. von Thunen, in the early nineteenth century on the basis of observations of his own Prussian estate. Set, like central place theory, in the context of neo-classical economics, whereby individual producers cannot affect the price of their commodities, it argued that the use of any piece of land would be a function of its productivity and the costs (borne by the producer) of transporting its output to the market. Assuming that land was equally productive for all commodities, the argument was that the greater the cost of transporting a particular product (because of its bulk and/or perishability) then, at a given price, the greater the benefit to the farmer of producing it close to the market. The economic rent yielded was then greatest at the market, and declined with distance from that point.

Two models were deduced from this theory: one, that there would be a zonal spatial organization of agricultural activities around a market; and the other, that the intensity of agricultural activity would decline (over all zones and also within each zone) with distance from the market. Again, such models provided a number of hypotheses which were amenable to testing.

Thunen's theory was also used as an analogy, as the model for the development of a theoretical structure regarding the organization of land-uses within an urban area. The work of Alonso, Muth, Wingo and others was based on this and, on the assumption of a monocentric urban area, produced the following testable hypotheses (*inter alia*): there is a zonal organization of land-uses around the centre of an urban area; land values decline with distance from the urban centre; and population densities decrease with distance from the city centre. All have been at least partially verified. (See Chisholm, 1979; Berry and Horton, 1970.)

Industrial location theory First expressed in the work of economists such as the German, Alfred Weber, and the American, Edgar Hoover, this theoretical structure was based on the initial assumption that all owners of manufacturing industries seek to locate their plants so as to minimize costs of production and of distribution to the market. Among these costs are those of transport, and so among the initial propositions was one that the location of manufacturing industry is undertaken so as to minimize transport costs. From such propositions, models of the distribution of industry could be developed, and hypotheses about particular locations could be derived. The body of theory was applied in a variety of contexts, increasingly emphasizing the importance of linkages between industries in the flow of goods, services and information, and the desire to maximize these links as a major influence on location. (See Lloyd and Dicken, 1978; Smith, 1981.)

Urban social areas Whereas the first three topics are concerned largely with economic geography, and derived their stimuli from work in economics and regional science, in the fourth the context was social and the main stimuli came from sociology, especially in the United States of America (where, in their turn, the sociologists were stimulated by an analogy between man/man and plant/plant – plant/environment interrelationships; through this analogy they developed the study of human ecology). The basic propositions were that society, especially advanced urban society, is divided into economic status groups (often termed classes), ethnic groups, and various interest groups and that members of these groups, for a variety of social and economic reasons, wish to live in separate parts of the urban area and to minimize inter-class and inter-group contacts. Distance was presented as a social rather than an economic barrier, therefore, although the two are obviously linked, and the groups compete for positions in urban space (just, according to the analogy, as plants do in any ecological situation). The spatial organization of urban residential areas reflects this use of distance as a social mechanism.

The model derived from this ecological theory had two components. The first was one of spatial congregation and segregation: like people tend to live together in the same areas, while unlike people live in separate areas. The second related to the morphology of this congregation and segregation: there is a particular spatial organization of cities with various social area types occupying particular type areas (inner city, outer suburb, etc.). Again, hypotheses could readily be derived from such models. (See Timms, 1971.)

Spatial interaction theory This final theoretical structure encompassed aspects of the other four, but was frequently treated separately. It focused on one aspect of the spatial organization of society – movement. Its basic initial proposition was that in any activity that involves movement, people seek to minimize the costs involved. Thus, the whole of the spatial organization of society involves an exercise in movement-minimization.

This thesis has a long history in the social sciences (Tocalis, 1968). Its development has been bolstered by an analogy with Newton's law of gravity, which relates interaction between two bodies with the product of their masses, and (inversely) with the distance separating them. Many hypotheses have been formulated and tested based on this 'gravity model': simply stated, they have claimed that the greater the distance between two places, the less the interaction between them.

Initially, this body of work focused largely on economic flows, of commodities and of people migrating between settlements, for example. But, as already indicated, the gravity-model thesis underlies most spatial science, and so it has been applied, in a catholic way, to movements of goods, people, capital, ideas etc. Associated with it has been the development of a body of theory regarding *spatial diffusion*, which argues that any innovation, including information and ideas, is spatially biased in its spread by the frictions of distance. Thus the general hypothesis developed that the further a person is from the source of a piece of information, the less likely he or she is to know of it, or the later that it reaches him or her; this has been applied in a variety of contexts (Cliff et al., 1981).

These five bodies of theory by no means encapsulate all of the work initially undertaken as part of the development of a positivist human geography. But the initial propositions outlined here were typical of much of the work. They illustrate how human geographers took certain basic ideas, mostly from other disciplines, and used them to develop models and hypotheses regarding patterns on the earth's surface (of settlements, as in central place theory, and of land-use types, as in agricultural location theory and the study of urban social areas) and regarding movements across that surface. Testing of those hypotheses involved the collection of data and the use of statistical procedures as verification methods (some of the modelling involved the use of mathematics). A large research literature has ensued. In addition, texts have been provided. Three types can be identified. The first (e.g. Haggett, 1965) seek to structure the content of human geography as a spatial science, emphasizing the relevant bodies of theory. The second (e.g. Abler, Adam and Gould 1971; Amedeo and Golledge, 1975) put greater emphasis on the positivist conception of science, as a means of doing geography within a contextual framework. And the third (e.g. Taylor, 1977) emphasize the techniques necessary for positivist work.

Problems of the positivist approach
In adopting the positivist conception of science, and applying it to human geography defined as spatial science, geographers encountered a number of problems, and also avoided tackling certain issues. Some of these problems and issues were general ones related to the relevance of a naturalistic, positivist methodology in social science, and thus the validity of the search for laws and theories. These major points were raised in critiques of the

positivist approaches and presentations of alternative philosophies of the social sciences (these are discussed in the remaining chapters of the book). Similarly, there were discussions of what has been termed the 'spatial separatist' theme (Sack, 1974), of whether a separate social science focusing on 'the spatial variable' is feasible (see Johnston, 1983a, Chapter 4); again this is discussed further in later chapters. But there have also been problems and issues within the positivist approaches themselves.

Behaviour and theory The first of these relates to the nature of the theory being developed in human geography. As already stressed most of this was derived from other disciplines, and much of it is rather informally structured (either it is expressed relatively imprecisely or, as Haynes 1975, 1977 argues, the formal structure of a mathematical theory may contain logical inconsistencies). A consequence of this has been that the hypotheses derived – via model-building in many cases – from the theories have proved to be relatively poor predictors. The theories have failed to provide convincing explanations; indeed, in some cases, notably central place theory, it has been shown that the initial assumptions of the theories have little basis in reality.

A strong argument in this context has been expressed with regard to those initial assumptions. The behaviourism underlying most of the bodies of theory outlined above has been of a normative form – this is how all people behave. Further, it is a particular type of normative assumption derived from neo-classical economics that states that, as an economic actor, man is an entirely rational profit-maximizer, which in a science of spatial relations means an entirely rational transport cost minimizer. (Some geographers seemed to believe that this is the only form of normative assumption. Any behaviour can be presented as normative, however – see Hay, 1979 – and can be the basis for theory articulation. The basic deductions of central place theory, for example, do not need every consumer to visit the nearest centre, only that there is no spatial variation in the proportion of consumers using the nearest, next nearest . . . etc. centre.) Because hypotheses were being falsified (when they should have been verified if the theory were to remain valid), this led to the argument that theories were being developed on false initial assumptions. New assumptions should be used, so the argument went, which were positive (what *is*) rather than normative (what *should be*; Pred. 1967, also argued that normative reasoning based on neo-classical economics was impossible).

This argument suggested the need for more direct observation of what people actually do, and how they reach their decisions. An inductive approach was therefore argued for. The result was a great deal of positive, behavourist work: empirical studies which sought to measure behaviour in terms of how it came about (though not why). Thus Golledge (1981, p. 1327) notes in reviewing such work that:

Researchers stressed that factors such as access to information, degree of risk aversion, images of environments, the stage of learning about stimulus situations, attitudes towards place, felt stress, risk aversion, place utility, and revealed preferences were important in understanding spatial activity.

The reaction to this was the development of what became known as 'behavioural geography' which was:

> process oriented. The processes emphasized . . . are human behavioral processes such as learning, perception, cognition, attitude formation, and so on . . . (p. 1327)

Data were collected from individual decision-makers regarding those process variables which it was assumed governed their behaviour: it did not focus on the unique individual but sought to generalize by aggregation of individuals, not in any *ad hoc* manner for its aim was:

> to *find* meaningful units of aggregation about which generalizations *can* be made (p. 1328)

(Note that Golledge's paper was in part a response to a critique by Bunting and Guelke, 1979. They claimed that behavioural work was based on two false assumptions: that identifiable environmental images exist which can be measured accurately, and that there are strong relationships between such images and behaviour. They suggest instead an idealist approach, see p. 52, based on the interpretation of overt behaviour.)

Central place theory, spatial interaction theory and the other elements of the 'new' geography of the 1950s and 1960s clearly influenced the selection of topics in 'behavioural geography' which focused on such issues as shopping centre choice, the decision to migrate and the search for a new home, choice of transport mode for a journey, and so on. The work was positivist in its search for generalizations through rigorous sampling procedures for data collection, measurement of both the attitudes and behaviour, and statement of the results. But it was not so explicitly theory-led, and hypotheses were not central to the research strategy in every case. This suggested inductivism to some (a charge also levelled at positivist work in general: Slater, 1973). The counter was that an inductive stage was a necessary precursor to the development of any viable theory, given the failings of the deductive theories with regard to explanation and prediction of behaviour. The failings, it was stressed, lay in the assumptions on which those theories were built:

> The examination of human actions required the definition of sets of assumptions . . . and the one most readily accepted was that of behavioural invariance . . . It was generally accepted that no proof of any of these assumptions was required, and it was not until behavioural work indicated the existence of substantial variability in perceptions and cognitions of external environments

and that different *spatial* behaviours could all be explained by the same decision process, that their shallowness was realized (Golledge, 1981, p. 1326)

As Golledge admits in the same review, no powerful new theory has emerged as a result of this behavioural work but he does claim 'substantial increments in the level of the understanding of human spatial activity' (p. 1339). The path to theory is a long one . . .

Verification Apart from the issues regarding behavioural assumptions underpinning geographical theories, substantial difficulties have been encountered in testing the validity of those being used. In brief, the problem can be reduced to the simple question 'What constitutes a verification of a geographical hypothesis?' (since almost all geographers ostensibly follow the verification rather than the falsification strategy). Answers to this question were never suggested, and just as Ayer could argue that many hypotheses are vaguely stated, so it could be suggested that many are vaguely tested. The criterion of verifiability, according to Ayer (1964, p. 35), is:

> We say that a sentence is factually significant to any given person, if, and only if, he knows how to verify the proposition which it purports to express — that is, if he knows what observations would lead him, under certain conditions to accept the proposition as being true, or reject it as being false.

Human geographers who take the positivist stance know that observations are needed, but have been far from clear as to the conditions for acceptance/rejection of a hypothesis: in commenting on this, Harvey (1969, p. 105) notes that:

> Statements derived from theory may turn out to be empirically insupportable, while empirical statements which intuitively appear to be of great significance sometimes cannot be linked to any existing theoretical structure . . . when we try to determine whether a particular statement is or is not a scientific law. The degree of theoretical support required, the degree of empirical support, the degree of confidence in the theoretical structure as a whole, and so on, may vary significantly from one person to another . . . The precise nature of the criteria may be obscure, but this does not mean that they are useless and insignificant.

For most human geographers using the positivist approach the criteria for hypothesis acceptance/rejection have been statistical, derived from the theories of probability. Thus, for example, if a correlation coefficient could be shown to be statistically significant at an (arbitrarily derived, usually 0.05) appropriate probability level, then this could be taken as evidence of the veracity of the hypothesis (assuming that the sign of the coefficient was as expected). As outlined above, the theory of probability can be used in two ways in such contexts. One states that the relationship observed in a sample is very likely to be present in the parent population (but at an unknown strength). The other states that in random orderings of the data set being studied, that particular relationship would occur only rarely by chance; since the relationship was predicted and is unlikely to occur by chance, it can be taken as 'real', and thus confirming the hypothesis.

Both of these approaches to statistical testing raise problems. With regard to the first, there are issues relating to the nature of the population and the sample. A hypothesis, and a theory from which it is drawn, must relate to a specified population from which a sample can be taken. What are the populations for geographical theories? They are far from clear in many cases. Thus what do the samples refer to? (Is a study of rural Wiltshire, comprising 200 settlements, a sample of *one* area in which central place theory is supposed to apply? Or is it a sample of 200 settlements, in which case it is surely not a properly constituted random sample?) If the nature of neither population nor sample is clear, then the validity of statistical significance tests must be very much in doubt.

If the sample-to-population approach to inferential statistics is invalid in much geographical work, then the reliance on probability theory must be based on the second of the ways outlined above. If this is so, then in each study the question being asked of the data is whether the expected relationship exists in that sample of one. (The expected relationship is usually vaguely stated. A correlation may be predicted; but how large? Or distance should have a negative exponent in a regression test of the gravity model; again, how large?) But if it is a sample of one, how far does it advance geographical knowledge if the finding is statistically significant? How many separate (independent) studies must report similar results before the hypothesis is verified? And if the studies are separate, do they together constitute a random sample of all possible studies?

The problems of verifying geographical hypotheses are considerable, therefore (more so, perhaps, than if the criterion of falsifiability were adopted). Because of this, although hypotheses derived from theories can be tested, the strategy of testing suggests that the accumulation of results may be little better than an inductive format. Whereas hypotheses in the natural sciences may be universal in their content, and can be tested in controlled conditions anywhere, many social scientific hypotheses are partial, and are set in contextual situations where proper experimentation is impossible. As such, the process of developing theories through contact with empirical reality is a slow one.

The geographical individual The third major problem stems from this. The subject matter of human geography is exceedingly complex; many laws are operating in the same place at the same time, under certain conditions. As a result, simple cause-effect hypotheses are difficult to isolate and test, because, as just suggested, it is not easy to abstract two elements only of a complex world and test for the postulated bivariate relationship. This was recognized early by geographers, who postulated multivariate hypotheses involving not only several independent variables acting on a dependent variable within a closed environment, but also those independent variables acting on each other, and thence on the dependent variable. Technical expertise was developed to handle such situations (Johnston, 1978) but a further problem was raised: can classical methods of inferential statistics be applied in spatial analysis? The problem of spatial autocorrelation raises a variety of technical and substantive issues. The technical issues, relating to the validity of inferential tests with data that are not from independent samples because the value of one is related to that of its neighbours, have been tackled (e.g. Cliff and Ord, 1980), but the substantive issues have been largely ignored, raising doubts in a few minds about the validity of many statistical analyses.

In much research, a further problem has been associated with defining the geographical individual, the focus of study. Few people have addressed this directly. An exception is Chapman's (1977) discussion of the entitiation problem, of the fact that 'Geography has consistently and dismally failed to tackle its entitiation problems, and that in that more than anything else lies the root of so many of its problems' (p. 7). The spectrum of objects available for study ranges from the atom, through the plant and animal to the nation and the world economy (which is a single unit). Somewhere along this continuum lies the geographer's object of study. Although he or she may collect data for, or use data collected from, individual units – be they people, shops or factories – the geographer is usually interested in some aggregation of these individuals, i.e. the population of a place (just, for example, as sociologists are interested in aggregations into classes and other groups). But what aggregation? As Chapman points out, the geographical concept of a region is somewhat vague, and gives little lead.

This issue of entitiation raises two problems. The first concerns populations and samples. If geographers are unsure what it is that they are studying, then this makes the design of experiments to test hypotheses extremely difficult. Secondly, there is the question of statistical validity. The results of, for example, a correlation analysis of the relationship between two variables is independent of neither the scale of the aggregation nor the actual aggregation at any particular scale. As Openshaw and Taylor (1980) have shown, the modifiable areal unit problem is such that with one data set (in this case the 99 counties of Iowa) it is possible to get a correlation between the percentage of the population aged over

60 of and the percentage voting Republican varying from + 0.999 to − 0.999 if the observations are aggregated into six 'regions' only, or between + 0.949 and − 0.745 if 36 'regions' are defined. (There is a very large number of ways in which 99 counties can be aggregated into 36 regions, let alone into six.) Which is the right correlation? If the geographer is not clear on the object he or she is studying, answering this question is virtually impossible.

Systems analysis

A major conceptual and technical issue that has faced human geographers wishing to apply the positivist conception of science to their discipline concerns the difficulties of articulating theory about, modelling, and experimenting on an exceedingly complex world organized by humans. The work discussed previously, on topics such as central place theory, presented and tested very simple hypotheses in the main, many of them straightforward cause-and-effect (or stimulus-response) sequences, involving single-cause models. Increasingly it was realized that the lack of convincing verification for these hypotheses reflected our over-simple view of reality, a belief that explanation could be advanced by the isolation of a very small section of the interrelationships that comprise the empirical world.

A realization that human geographers needed to tackle the complexity of their subject matter was associated with a developing interest in *systems*. Simply defined, a system is a set of elements, each with certain attributes, that are linked together in a particular way. Activation of the links (flows of some type between elements) operates the system, so that the analogy between system and organism (see p. 7) is a close one. The nature of the links between the elements governs not only the operation of the system but also, where relevant, its evolution. Processes of change are built into the system.

Any system is a simplification, since it represents an abstraction of a part of reality from its encompassing environment (which might be represented as other systems). The justification for any system is that it is relatively self-contained and thus presents a sensible focus for study. Links between the system and its environment will probably activate it, and in turn the system may deliver certain outputs to the environment. As such, the concept of a system has been advanced as a valuable perspective on the complexity of those aspects of reality studied by human geographers (see Bennett and Chorley, 1978).

The argument for the systems approach has been made by several writers, including Harvey (1969, Chapter 23). One of the strongest advocates has been Chorley, who has argued that, among other things, it provides a valuable means for integrating human and physical geography. By focusing on systems of interrelated components, which interact on each other, rather than producing simple cause-and-effect hypotheses:

> systems methods have illuminated thought, clarified objectives and cut through the theoretical and technical undergrowth (Bennett and Chorley, 1978, p. 540).

(Some geographers were attracted by general systems analysis which, in line with the positivist view on the unity of science, proposes that there are considerable similarities between the organization of many types of systems, and that investigation of these could well provide useful analogies for the study of geographical systems: see Chisholm, 1967; Harvey, 1969.)

Fundamental to the systems approach is the modelling stage of the positivist procedures, for the aim of systems analysis is to provide a faithful representation of the interactions within a system rather than to extract a few simple relationships that can be submitted to empirical testing procedures. (A full description of systems modelling is Huggett, 1980.) Such modelling recognizes that most interrelationships are not of the simple form $B = f(A)$, which states that the value of B is a function of the value of A, unless an over-simplified abstraction is to be undertaken. A system could well be structured in the following sequence (i.e. they operate after one another in time):

$$B = f(A)$$
$$C = f(B)$$
$$A = f(C)$$
$$D = f(C)$$
$$B = f(D)$$

which is represented diagrammatically in Figure 1.

If a simple hypothesis were to be extracted from this sequence it might well postulate a linear relationship between B as the dependent variable and A as the independent. This could be tested, using the positivist procedures. But by embedding that relationship in the structure of five equations which describes the entire functioning of the system, it is possible to realize that, in effect, $A = f(A)$, mediated through B and C. (In addition, D influences A through B and C, so that $A = f(A)$ is not a complete statement.) This is a feedback effect, with the state of A at one time partly influencing its state at the next.

The advantages claimed for the systems approach are several. First, by studying wholes rather than parts of wholes – the operation of an entire system rather than a few elements of it – geographical study is more realistic. From this, secondly, flows the argument that explanation is more comprehensive, because it is all-encompassing. Thus:

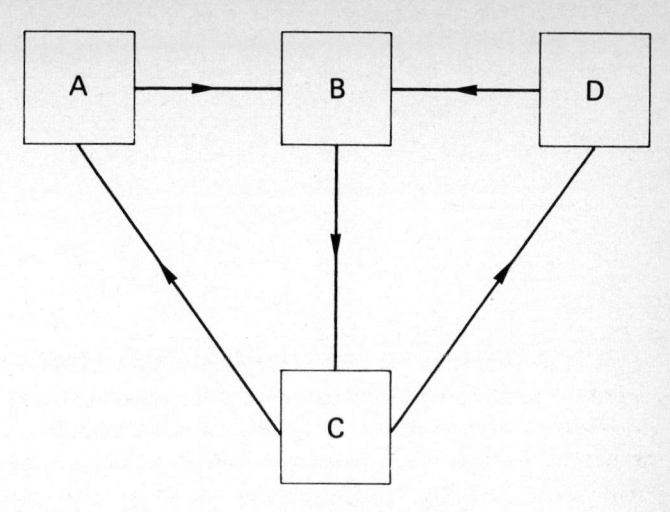

[Figure 1: Diagram showing boxes A, B, D at top with C at bottom; arrows A→B, D→B, B→C, C→A, C→D]

Figure 1

whatever our philosophical views may be, it has been shown that methodologically the concept of the system is absolutely vital to the development of a satisfactory explanation Harvey, 1969, p. 479)

And finally, stemming from more satisfactory explanation, is the greater utility of the output. If systems analysis in geography can provide better predictions and explanations than the other applications of the positivist conception of science, then it is providing better tools for manipulating systems – for social control.

Within human geography, attempts to introduce systems analysis and the modelling of complex inter-relationships have characterized certain areas of economic geography, notably those concerned with economic growth in an international, regional, or urban context. (A good example is the work of Pred, 1977, on the dynamics of urban growth, whose basis lies in the input-output formulation of the structure of an economy. His initial statements showed that urban growth becomes self-generating because of the nature of the system. Expansion in one industry in a town generates expansion in others through the extra purchasing power that it provides and its increased demands for the products of other industries; such first-round expansion generates even more in a second round – the other industries in turn contribute extra purchasing power to the local economy – and so on. In later work, he showed how such self-generating growth favours certain places – mainly the large ones – and discriminates against others, leading to alterations in the relative importance of settlements within the regional or national system.) Much of this work on systems has stopped at the model-building stage, because of problems of obtaining data to test the models as wholes rather than as series of separate hypotheses. (For some examples, see Bennett and Chorley, 1978.) But the introduction of a systems approach has led to considerable acquisition of technical expertise by the discipline.

Systems of linked equations, such as those above, raise a number of problems in calibration (fitting them to data), especially if understanding of the system is incomplete and data are not available for all of the links. Thus the equations above (Figure 1) included:

$$B = f(A)$$
$$C = f(B)$$
$$A = f(C)$$

which could be simplified to $A = f(A)$, except that it must be made clear that $A_t = f(A_{t-x})$, which states that the value of A at time t is a function of the value of A at a previous time $(t - x)$, x units earlier. (It could be extended to $A_t = f(A_{t-x}, A_{t-2x}, \ldots)$.) Such a relationship is sometimes termed a 'black box', and sometimes as *instrumentalism* (Gregory, 1980). The investigator knows that A affects something else, which in turn affects A; he cannot isolate that 'something else' so merely calibrates a model which says that A affects A (somehow) and which provides him with a predictive device for estimating/forecasting future values of A. (For an introduction, see Bennett, 1979.)

A major input to geography as spatial science has been the introduction of spatial components to systems analysis. Derived in particular from work on spatial interaction – especially with regard to diffusion (see above, p. 35) – geographers have argued that not only is:

$$A_t = f(A_{t-x})$$

which states that the value of A at time t at any point is a function of an earlier value of A there, but also:

$$A_{it} = f(A_{jt-x})$$

where the value of A at place i at time t is also a function of the value at place j at time $t - x$; the nature of the function – the degree to which the value at j influences the value at i – is usually assumed to relate to the distance between the two points i and j. Addition of a spatial to a temporal component extends the equations to:

$$A_{it} = f\left(\sum_{k=1}^{x} A_{i, t-k}\right) + f\left(\sum_{j=1}^{n} \sum_{k=1}^{x} A_{j, t-k}\right)$$

in which the value of A at place i and time t is a function of its value there at each preceding time (x units of length k: the first term of the equation) and at each preceding time at each other place (n) in the system (the second term in the equation). Such a systems model can be used to represent spatial variations in prices at agricultural markets, for example, with the price at one market being related both to the price there at previous dates and the price at adjacent markets, with the influence of the latter reflecting their distance from the market being studied (Martin and Oeppen, 1975). Calibrating such equations (i.e. fitting them to data) is technically demanding on data (Bennett, 1979b).

The systems approach is one, therefore, in which *the entire model is the hypothesis* rather than the source of separate hypotheses. As such, it offers a greater stimulus to the explanation of events because of its more holistic approach. Because of its technical problems, however, its application has not been widespread. This is particularly so if the models are not deterministic, so that they can only provide conditional predictions – because of either incomplete specification or randomness as an element in the system. Thus any realization – the actual pattern in the world – is but one of a very large number: from this, Chapman (1977) argues that a system is a set of objects for which a large number of potential states is feasible, and that the task for a human geographer involves identifying the nature of that feasible set and the likelihood of the observed situation arising. This approach has been taken furthest by Wilson (1970) in his work on traffic flows, which uses certain information about the system (where the workers live, where the jobs are, what the transport links are) to provide a best-estimate of 'unknowns' about the system (the commuting flows). His model is thus a prediction which can be tested. If it is a weak prediction (again, the problems of what is a satisfactory verification are paramount) he returns to the model and recalibrates it to try and improve its fit.

The systems approach makes more explicit the naturalistic assumption underlying the positivist conception of social science. Systems of interest to human geographers are treated *as if they were machines*, comprising linked working parts which have little or no independent existence and whose positions in the system are predetermined. This is associated with the structural-functionalist approach to sociology advanced by Merton (1957). According to this, a system (e.g. a society, or component of a society such as an individual organization) comprises a set of elements, each of which has a fixed place and function related to the system's goals. The nature of the system is fixed, therefore, and should be dissected readily. Also fixed is its dynamic of change. The relationship between elements may not be unalterable. The changes that occur result from the operations of the system itself (which may be exceedingly complex, as recent mathematical work in human geography has indicated: Wilson, 1981), however, so that change results from the operation of internal, not external, forces. Identification of the forces for change provides a basis for even more sophisticated systems' control, and is the goal of work on the research frontier.

Positivism and logical positivism in human geography
Much of the preceding discussion has been based on the assumption that human geographers have been practising – or seeking to practise – as positivists; they have been aiming to develop generalizations and laws within a philosophical framework initiated by Comte. (Such an assumption has been made by others – e.g. Gregory, 1978a – who criticize positivist work in human geography.) But whereas many human geographers in the 1950s and 1960s were attracted to a positivistic position – in particular to its emphasis on precision via quantification – they were not adopting the entire positivist package and were not applying the full methodology as presented by Harvey (1969). If this was so, then all human geographers were doing was to use part of the positivist package in order to present more rigorous descriptions. Furthermore, they were not embracing the full 'scientism' package of logical positivism (see. p. 13).

This case has been made by several authors in the early 1980s as part of a defence against anti-positivist critiques. The burden of the argument is that 'we are positivist but not logical positivist'. Thus Golledge (1981), in responding to Bunting and Guelke (1979), argues that:

> there are substantial differences between the philosophy of logical positivism and a positivist philosophy. The latter, although entrenched firmly in scientific procedures is nowhere as epistemologically constrained as logical positivism (p. 1333).

He does not indicate the nature of the constraints, however, but quotes Entrikin (1976) as his source. The latter states that:

> Scientific geography can be quite broadly defined as an approach based upon empirical observation, public verifiability of conclusions and the importance of isolating fact from value (p. 616).

and

> description, explanation, and prediction are important aspects of the scientific method (p. 631).

These quotations imply that in a positivist philosophy – which is not logical positivism – the goal of prediction follows from achievement of precise description and verifiable explanation. As pointed out above (p. 13) this incorporates much of the 'positivist conception of science' (or 'scientific method') which was codified by the logical positivists and it makes no reference to the elimination of metaphysics (p. 13). It differs from the positivist conception of science only in the absence of any reference to hypotheses. Since, as also indicated above (p. 37), Golledge indicates that eventually his scientific study of behaviour should lead to the development of theory (which will presumably be a source of hypotheses), it is difficult to see in what way this differs from most positivistic geography. If the argument is that you can be scientific without being a full logical positivist, most human geographers would undoubtedly agree with Golledge. It is not clear what else he is asking for.

A somewhat similar argument to Golledge's has been made by Bennett (1981a; see also Bennett and Wrigley, 1981). He claims that Harvey's (1969) presentation of logical positivism as applied to human geography 'is only a partial representation of the literature and ideas it seeks to describe' (p. 13) and that Gregory's (1978a, 1980) criticism of 'theoretical and quantitative geography' in the context of instrumentalism and social engineering is 'both superficial and inexact' (p. 14):

> the critique has been directed at an abstract and misrepresented view of much of quantitative geography, one which attributes methods, views, and conclusions to quantitative geographers which most have never held, or if they did ever hold, have since abandoned, or if they still hold in some form, hold only in part alongside wider views (p. 14).

The view which Bennett is contesting is one which proposes 'that quantitative geography is alienating in distracting researchers from the central question of social distribution' (p. 12). He identifies five elements to this view: positivist work creates a false sense of objectivity which leads to an ability to manipulate society ('scientific politics' according to Keat, see p. 13); quantification and the associated computing technology dehumanizes man; because it is descriptive of society, positivist work must support the status quo of that society, especially its future; positivist work contains no values about how society should be organized; and positivism seeks universal generalizations inductively. He argues that such criticism 'has had a pernicious and distractive effect' and 'has suggested that scientific and empirical enquiry is largely socially worthless' (p. 24).

The arguments presented by Golledge and, especially, by Bennett therefore suggest that empirical, descriptive work that is scientifically rigorous can be conducted outside the positivist context: it may be atheoretical, therefore, in that it is not explicitly theory-led (although any selection of what to study, and how, involves an implicit theory, and a philosophy); and it may be descriptive but perhaps not predictive (i.e. law-like, it merely states something precisely). Such work is basically empiricist: within geography it is more rigorous (i.e. quantitative) than in the empiricist regional and systematic studies it sought to replace. Logical positivism is both philosophy and ideology, and is rejected by most human geographers. Positivism (or scientific method) is methodology and technology. To Bennett, it seems, it is the latter but not the former.

Bennett, like Golledge, appears to be defending a stance of 'We are positivist, but not logical positivist'. To the extent that relatively few human geographers argued in the heady days of the 1950s and 1960s for scientism and scientific politics, and even fewer do now, this is undoubtedly so. Human geographers sought to study certain subject matter scientifically, which they interpreted as rigorously. But Bennett appears to go further than this. He notes that Johnston (1983a, 1980b) presents Harvey's codification of the positivist approach to science 'without criticism'. As argued above, however, adoption of the positivist methodology does not necessarily imply adoption of logical positivism (although Johnston's first edition, 1979, p. 63, falsely equates the two). Thus Bennett would seem to be arguing that 'quantitative geographers' were not only not logical positivists but also that they were not positivists. (It is true, of course, that many pieces were at best 'quantitative empiricism' and that the logic of their analysis did not follow the model-hypothesis-test-law sequence. It could be argued, however, that such description is a necessary precursor to work in that sequence.)

Certainly a considerable volume of literature produced by human geographers in the 1960s and 1970s fits into this 'quantitative empiricist' categorization. Disillusionment with the available theories and models, such as those described above (pp. 25–31), led to the development of the 'positivist behaviouralism' (p. 37) that comprised quantitative description and analysis in something of an atheoretical vacuum. Industrial geographers, for example, abandoned the location theories that were the catalyst for work in the early 1960s and turned instead to descriptive analyses of, for example, the desertion of the inner city by manufacturing industry and the impacts of government regional policies on the distribution of industrial employment (e.g. Keeble, 1976). Such work was more *ad hoc* and pragmatic than that done within the context of industrial location theory. Its hypotheses (if any were stated) were not deeply embedded in theory and its aims were not phrased in terms of laws. But in some cases at least utility was sought, in that the analysts were describing what was happening and evaluating certain policies as part of a more general monitoring of social and economic policy (and indeed some were doing their research under contract from government departments). Utility implies *la certitude*.

Such 'empiricist/positivist' work can be identified in many subfields of human geography, especially in the literature of the 1970s. Evaluations, especially with regard to the quantitative methods used, stress the limited goal of rigorous description. With regard to factor analysis, for example, Taylor (1981, p. 251) claims that it is:

> best considered as simply a measurement technique.

but he also points out that:

> any research employing this tool is ultimately to be assessed not on technical grounds but in terms of the overall social model underlying the research.

All description, however sophisticated, must be theoretically led. In much human geography it may have been that the theory was implicit, or even poorly understood by the researcher. In political geography, for example, it has been realized that a neutral science is not possible (Johnston, 1981b); nor is it atheoretical. In his book *The Geography of Public Finance* Bennett (1980) presents the subject matter as:

> *who gets what* benefits from public finance as a function of *where* the individual lives and *where* the industrial enterprise is located (p. 1).

This would appear to call for a descriptive exercise, but his description is led by a model:

> Much of the book is concerned with the issue of equity (p. 6) . . . Public finance in general and in its geographical components in particular, is aimed at eliminating, or at least reducing, the unequal treatment of individuals in society (p. 17).

and this model is clearly one with normative as well as positive ends: it seeks to prescribe as well as to describe, as illustrated by Bennett's (1981b) application of control theory to suggest an optimal distribution of central government grants in England and Wales.

The attempts to separate quantitative work from positivism suggest that scientific rigour in description and analysis can be undertaken in a theoretically agnostic framework which pays little attention to one or more of theories, hypotheses, laws, predictions and applications. Undoubtedly some human geographers have worked in this way and have sought to provide rigorous descriptions only. But, as Taylor (1981) points out with regard to the use of factorial ecology in the study of urban social areas:

> any technique is only as good as researchers will allow it to be. The most important element of any research design is the social theory in which it is embedded. Unfortunately it is just this feature that is typically ignored as it appears in the undiscussed assumptions of the research (p. 257).

No description can be atheoretical, for its terminology alone is theoretically defined. Nor, if it relates to contemporary material, can it be divorced from its potential use to manipulate society. Knowledge is theoretically produced and is theoretically (or ideologically) employed. Thus quantitative geographers may dissociate themselves not only from logical positivism in particular but also, in some cases, from positivism in general. As such their work may be presented as empiricist. Because of the emphasis on quantitative rigour, it could be termed logical empiricism (see Passmore, 1957), although this term is also applied to logical positivism by some (see p. 12 above). But 'pure' empiricism is not possible, for ideas must be derived from a theoretical base, however weak, and methods too cannot readily be dissociated from a philosophy. Thus much human geography work is undoubtedly positivist in conception and execution, and the separate, apparently empiricist, pieces are the building-blocks for the positivist programmes. In Rudner's (1966) terms, they are undertaken in the 'context of discovery' which must be followed, if firm generalizations are to be made, by the 'context of verification', which involves the positivist conception of science.

Summary

The positivist conception of science is a particular approach to knowledge based on clearly-defined epistemological and ontological positions. Its epistemology – its statements regarding the nature of knowledge and how it can be obtained – is based on the evidence of experience and how that evidence is obtained; explanation of the world is to be achieved via structured (i.e. theory-led) observation of the world. Its ontology – its statements of what exists – backs this up, with arguments that only what is directly observable (and measurable, to many) is acceptable as evidence. Its methodolgy is the hypothetico-deductive progress towards explanation, with its emphasis on verification in replicable 'experiments' as the only evidence of the veracity of hypotheses.

The validity of such a philosophy for natural sciences is clear. Theories about nature can be developed, models of particular aspects of it built, hypotheses about certain relationships derived, and experiments designed to test their validity. Successful experiments, properly conducted and reported so that other scientists will accept their findings, have two outcomes. First, they increase the store of knowledge, of information structured in such a way that it can be related to other information: they provide the basis for universal laws and general theories. Secondly, they provide the means of predicting, of saying what will happen next in certain circumstances. This allows not only foresight but also manipulation. If one knows that to do something will produce something else, then one may be able to avoid the latter if it is unwanted or to produce it if it is desired.

The attractions of this conception to the social sciences are that it can advance explanation, providing knowledge of society rather than accumulations of fact. It can predict, which gives society foresight about itself. And it can provide the means for social control, for engineering society towards certain ends. In addition, there are many other, lesser features which appeal to social scientists, such as the ability to make valid statements about behaviour. Thus the positive social science advocated by Comte in the nineteenth century has become increasingly attractive, not only to those social scientists who have sought to advance knowledge, their disciplines, and themselves, but also to the employers of social scientists, who have perceived the potential of obtaining useful information.

In human geography, as outlined here, the adoption of the positivist conception of science after the Second World War led to a major reorientation of geographical work. Certain aspects of the approach were emphasized – such as measurement, data collection, and the statistical testing of hypotheses – whereas others were relatively ignored. The result has been a great volume of work seeking to establish relationships in space, to display the correlations between distributions and to account for the characteristics of particular places in the light of those correlations. In terms of knowledge – as against information – the value of much of this work is questioned by some, because of its lack of theoretical articulation and its apparent irrelevance to real explanation. (To others, as indicated above, this is seen as a benefit.) Technically, work has become much more sophisticated in a short space of time. Substantively, a large number of topics have been tackled. Description is precise, but has understanding been advanced far?

The problems of the positivist approaches to geography are grouped into two categories. The first reflect Keat's (1981) list of positivist claims discussed above. Is the positivist conception of science the only approach to knowledge? Does positivism offer rational solutions to social problems? And is positivism value free? The second group, linked to these, relates to epistemology and ontology. Is experience (structured via experiment) the only means of knowing? Is the phenomenal environment the only source of evidence for explanation? Is explanation feasible? Are mechanistic models valid for the study of man? Is social control via science desirable? The philosophy which human geographers have adopted is that of the positivist conception of science. The philosophy of logical positivism is that knowledge is only attainable in this way. Although human geographers have in general not accepted the latter, it is still possible to ask whether the subject matter that they have studied positivistically is properly studied in that way. Is too much human geography set in the positivist mould? Should any of it be?

3
Humanistic approaches

The basic feature of humanistic approaches is their focus on man as a thinking being, as a human, rather than as a dehumanized responder to stimuli in some mechanical way, which is how some feel man is presented in the positivist and structuralist social sciences. There is a variety of such approaches, for which there is no agreed collective noun. Their common element is a stress on the study of man as he is, by a researcher who has as few presuppositions as possible. The aim is to identify the true nature of human action, and this end, and the means proposed to achieve it, represents the development of philosophies of and for the social sciences, rather than the adoption of philosophies developed for other realms of investigation.

Varieties of humanistic research

There is a wide variety of humanistic approaches within the social sciences, which differ in many ways but which are in general agreement about the main subject matter of the social sciences: the subjectivity of both observer and observed. Their goal is to examine that subjectivity (especially that of the observed); the exact nature of that goal and the means by which it can be pursued have been the subject of considerable debate, both between and within the major humanistic schools. This chapter, like the previous one, does not set out to review the history and nature of those debates in any detail. Rather it is a presentation of the major elements of three main humanistic approaches, which in varying degrees have all been presented as relevant to work in human geography.

Idealism

Idealism is a philosophy with a long history and deep tradition. Its basic tenet, that all reality is in some way a mental construction so that the world does not exist outside its observation and representation by man, has long been posed against the positivist epistemology and its emphasis on objective evidence. To some, as Ewing (1934) points out, idealism involves the belief that the ordering of the universe by man is determined by spiritual values. This he claims is a restricted definition, however – idealism embraces a wider range of philosophies that:

have in common the view that there can be no physical objects existing apart from some experience, and this might perhaps be taken as the definition of idealism, provided we regard thinking as a part of experience and do not imply by 'experience' passivity, and provided we include under experience not only human experience but . . . the experience of a God (p. 3).

This requires a definition of physical objects. Ewing argues that the position ascribed to an idealist depends on the acceptance of one or more of the following three arguments:

(a) because of a general theory of knowledge which implies that no object can exist apart from a knowing mind, (b) because he holds that the particular characteristics of matter logically imply an experiencing or thinking mind, or (c) because he holds that physical objects, while not implying a mind on which they depend, are themselves of the nature of experience or are physical entities of some kind (p. 5).

According to the idealist view, therefore, man builds up his own picture of the world, within which his actions are predicated. The nature of that picture is to some extent determined by the purpose for which it is being constructed, but:

we are active in cognition and never arrive at a fact merely by sensation or by passively receiving data but always understand it in terms of preconceived, though not usually explicitly formulated, theories . . . We cannot . . . apprehend the real without thought (Ewing, 1934, p. 235).

Man, as an active being, develops theories to guide his action. Such guidance includes the direction of future thinking, the interpretation of perceptions, and the nature of decision-making. The theories are developed inductively, by a learning process in which new knowledge is incorporated within theories.

For theories to be developed, and for evidence to be assessed and interpreted, criteria must be used. Central to idealism, therefore, is its coherence theory, which includes: a definition of truth; an account of the nature of reality; and a criterion of truth (Ewing, 1934, p. 195). To positivists, a proposition is correct when it accords with the objective evidence; to idealists it is correct when it coheres with accepted theories. Coherence implies a systematic view of the world:

(a) that everything is causally determined; (b) that everything is, directly or indirectly, causally connected with everything else, so that there is no series of events in the universe which is causally independent of all events outside that series; (c) that the relation of causality involves a relation of logical entailment, so that whatever is causally impossible is also logically impossible relatively to the rest of the causal system (Ewing, 1934, p. 231).

Thus all new knowledge must fit into the orbit of existing theory – it must be logically related to it – because that theory is of an interdependent world. Eventually, therefore, for a theory to be coherent it must be comprehensive. This, however, is a goal to be sought rather than a reality – en route:

> To assert separately from the rest is not to deny the rest (Ewing, 1934, p. 234).

Theories are built up (and if necessary modified) through learning; because knowledge within a theory must cohere, the test of a theory lies in a dilemma: 'Believe this or believe nothing'. One holds on to a belief until it appears that holding such a belief creates incoherence in theories of other parts.

Idealism, then, is a philosophy which proposes that knowledge is entirely subjective. It is ordered by individuals according to their own theoretical systems, which are modified in the light of new knowledge but whose criterion of truth is internal to the theory – 'Does it all fit together?' – rather than external to it. To study human decision-making, according to this view, involves studying the decision-makers and the personal theories that guided them.

This idealist philosophy has received favour among some historians, who have argued against the positivist view, which to some suggests a pre-determined plan by which history unfolds, if it is to be subject to laws and generalizations. Thus, according to Collingwood (1965, p. 36):

> The plan which is revealed in history is a plan which does not pre-exist prior to its own revelation; history is a drama, but an extemporised drama, co-operatively extemporised by its own performers.

Pursuing this analogy, Collingwood argues that every piece of history has its own plot, and it is the task of the historian to discover that plot:

> To look for a plot in history means seeing history in its individuality, seeing every incident in it as an irreplaceable and unique element in an irreplaceable and unique whole; whereas looking in history for instances of general laws means failing to group the individuality of history and seeing every incident in it as a more reduplication of a ready-made type, and the whole as a chaotic assemblage of such reduplications (Collingwood, 1965, p. 210).

Collingwood's philosophy of history, therefore, is of a discipline which:

> seeks to study the activities of the human spirit not by setting up imaginary instances of them, like the artist, nor yet by substituting for them a mechanical play of abstract types, like the psychologist, but by apprehending them in their full actuality (p. 47).

He studies human decision-making as the outcome of individual theories.

In Collingwood's philosophy of history, idealism refers not only to the objects of the historian's study but also to the individual historian. He, too, is developing personal theories of past events, assimilating new knowledge and applying a coherence theory and its criterion of truth as the method of assessing interpretations: 'Does it all fit together?' In part he must do this because of the lack of certainty about historical 'facts'. The historian erects a skeleton of theory:

> some working hypothesis as to the things especially worth noticing, especially crucial in their revelation of the nature of the process in which they occur. In reality . . . history has no skeleton; when we fully understand any historical event, each element in it appears as crucial as the rest; but the optical illusion that it has a skeleton is inevitably generated by our own ignorance (p. 39).

The skeleton is always likely to be present however. Indeed, there will be many skeletons, representing the views of individual historians, all exercising individual judgement on the information available to them and how it fits with their interpretations and reconstructions of the events of earlier periods. Thus:

> Everyone brings his own mind to the study of history . . . The attempt to eliminate this 'subjective element' from history is always insincere – it means keeping your own point of view while asking other people to give up theirs – and always unsuccessful (p. 138).

Collingwood's philosophy of history, therefore, is one based on what he calls the historical imagination. Each event in the past has what he calls an outside and an inside (Collingwood, 1946, p. 213). The outside comprises the observable conditions relating to it, whereas the inside involves the thoughts behind it. An historian must study both:

> His work may begin by discovering the outside of an event, but it can never end there; he must always remember that the event was an action, and that his main task is to think himself into this action, to discern the thought of its agent (Collingwood, 1946, p. 213).

The study of history, then, involves 'knowledge of mind', which involves the historian putting himself in the context of the relevant actors so that he can re-enact both the thought and the action.

This idealist history is more than what Collingwood terms 'commonsense history', which is based on memory and authority: memory involves the statements of the actors, as in the various surviving texts; authority implies that the memory is believed. But the historian must not take such statements at their face value. He must subject them to criticism, testing the extent to which they fit into his 'web of imaginative construction', his theory of how and why the actors did what they did. To stress this point, Collingwood draws an analogy between historians and novelists, and uses a detective story as illustration:

> Each of them makes it his business to construct a picture which is partly a narrative of events, partly a description of situations, exhibition of motives,

analysis of characters. Each aims at making his picture a coherent whole . . . The novel and the history must both of them make sense . . . Where they . . . differ is that the historian's picture is meant to be true (Collingwood, 1946, pp. 245-246).

To approach truth, the historian is constrained by three rules: the subject matter must be localized in place and time; the pieces must be consistent with one another; and the construction must be consistent with the available evidence.

Idealist history involves the reconstruction of the context of actions. The historian rethinks the thoughts of his subjects, in a way which is consistent both with his conception of the whole of which those thoughts are a part and with the available evidence. On these criteria, it is argued, all inquiries are historical, whether they are concerned with the individual seeking to reconstruct his own ideas or with the study of others. Once performed, all human action is history, and it can only be accounted for by application of the idealist method and the exercise of the historical imagination.

Phenomenology and its relations
Phenomenology is a philosophy of science based on the same foundations as idealism: all knowledge is subjective. It seeks to analyse and identify the basic features of subjective knowledge, not only to provide an understanding of man but also in the practical sense of 'making life itself more significant' (Spiegelberg, 1976, p. 79) by uncovering its meanings and values. Thus its:

> primary objective is the direct investigation and description of phenomena as consciously experienced, without theories about their causal explanation and as free as possible from unexamined preconceptions and presuppositions (Spiegelberg, 1975, p. 3).

The development of phenomenology is associated with the pioneering work of the German philosopher Edmund Husserl (see Farber, 1943). This was based on earlier conceptions of how to study the subjective and spawned a wide range of positions which are generally accepted as phenomenological (see the listing in Spiegelberg, 1975, p. 10; also Wolff, 1979). The common ground to such work includes:

1 The belief that man should be studied free of any preconceived theories or suppositions about how he acts. The observer's view of the world should be suspended (put into abeyance – Husserl's term for this is *bracketing*), so that interpretations are not contaminated by concepts and potential explanations that are alien to the subject.

2 The search for understanding (represented by the German word *verstehen* – see below) or appreciation of the nature of an act as the goal of social science, rather than for explanation (the term associated with positivism and its emphasis on objective evidence).

3 The belief that for man the world exists only as a mental construction, created in acts of *intentionality*. An element is brought into an individual's world only when he or she gives it meaning because of some intention towards it.

The goal of phenomenology, then, is to reconstruct the worlds of individuals, the phenomena in those worlds which are there as repositories of meaning. This leads to an understanding of behaviour in those worlds, which is not the same as a positivist's explanation, since the latter is a construct imposed by the analyst whereas an understanding uses the terms and concepts of the actor (Entrikin, 1976). But the nature of that reconstruction enterprise varies considerably, and has led Spiegelberg (1975, pp. 15-16) to recognize five types of phenomenology:

1 *Descriptive phenomenology* – the presentation of material (phenomena) in the life-worlds of the individuals studied.
2 *Essential phenomenology* – the identification of essences (the essential characteristics or meanings) of phenomena. This (sometimes known as eidetic intuition) involves moving beyond the surface manifestations of the allocation of meanings to the underlying processes involved, studying:

> experiences that can be analyzed in intuition in their essential generality and not . . . experiences as real occurrences in the natural world (Farber, 1943, p. 211).

General essences, then, are universals built up from particular examples (such as colour). Particulars can then be studied as examples of such generalities (with the relationship being defined by the subject and not by the observer). From this, the phenomenologist can then move to the apprehension of essential relationships, the articulation within and between general essences, and the ways in which subjective theories are developed.
3 *The phenomenology of appearances* – the study of how essences take shape, as intentionality operates and meanings are assigned.
4 *Constitutive phenomenology* – essences, and essential relationships, develop as patterns that become part of consciousness. Constitutive phenomenology studies how such consciousness develops.
5 *Hermeneutic phenomenology* – the interpretation of meanings which are concealed in consciousness and which are 'not immediately manifest to our intuiting, analyzing and describing' (Spiegelberg, 1976, p. 695).

Not all phenomenologists, Spiegelberg argues, either accept or practise all five of these. Many practise descriptive and essential phenomenology only, arguing that the other three are impossible tasks, since the observer cannot enter into the mind of the subject. These arguments are particularly relevant to the adoption of phenomenology in certain social sciences (notably sociology – see below).

The focus of phenomenology, therefore, is the understanding of human action through the study of meanings allocated to the elements of the individual's life-world. This is not subjective empiricism, however, for it is founded on the belief that such meanings, the characteristics ascribed by individuals, including practising scientists, to phenomena, are the products of general essences that exist within human consciousness, and which – some phenomenologists believe – can themselves be appreciated. Further, the aim of phenomenology is not only to understand but, by understanding, to enrich life by increasing human awareness. Thus:

> the phenomenological approach is opposed to exploratory hypotheses: it confines itself to the direct evidence of intuitive seeing . . . it constitutes a determined attempt to enrich the world of our experience by bringing out hitherto neglected aspects of this experience . . . [displaying] an omniverous desire for variety . . . [or] unusually obstinate attempt to look at the phenomena and to remain faithful to them before even thinking about them (Spiegelberg, 1976, p. 700).

It begins, therefore, by the study of the 'natural attitude', the life-world which individuals accept and live in, without questioning, although in all encounters with elements there may be suspicion. Having identified the contents of the natural attitude, it then seeks to articulate the general essences that underlie it and, from those, the absolute knowledge that resides in consciousness.

As to phenomenological method, this is frequently summarized by a phrase of Husserl's – 'to the things' – interpreted as implying that phenomena (i.e. the meanings given to items in the individual's life-world) must be transmitted to the phenomenologist without intermediaries. Access must be gained to the subject's life-world, therefore. As Spiegelberg (1975, p. 46) recognizes, complete access to the subject's mind is impossible, but:

> This does not mean that our perception of other selves is infallible. It may be subject to the usual, plus some unusual, illusions to which all uncritical, and perhaps even some critical, perception is exposed. All the same, here is the only possible gateway to all knowledge of others.

Several routes to this gateway are suggested by Spiegelberg. It may be possible, for example, for a trained observer to identify (perhaps by inference) certain feelings, and thus meanings, in the subject's actions: this raises the problem, however, that 'We may see his eyes as seeing but we cannot see what it is that he sees through these eyes' (Spiegelberg, 1975, p. 46). Thus, bracketing may not be achieved by the observer. Nevertheless, because we cannot see through the eyes of others, approximate solutions to that problem must be found. Spiegelberg suggests two.

The first of these phenomenological methods is *imaginative self-transposal*, which:

> requires that the investigator imagines himself as occupying the real place of the other and view from there the world as it would present itself in this new perspective . . . [the investigator] adapts imaginatively as much as . . . [he or she] can of the frame of mind of the other person. Clues for this adoption are to be derived from firsthand perception of the other and from facts of his available biography . . . the ability to vary oneself in imagination is easily one of the most remarkable capacities of the human self (Spiegelberg, 1975, pp. 48–49).

Thus, it is suggested, essential insights can be achieved by vicarious imagination rather than by perception, by the observer attempting to translate himself into the subject's situation and from that position reconstructing his or her life-world. The method is reflective.

The second method is *co-operative encounter and exploration*, a procedure associated with Freud's psychoanalysis. Subject and analyst embark on a joint exploration of the former's life-world, in a relationship of mutual trust and respect. Within this, the subject:

> by putting his [i.e. the subject's] own perspective – to the best of his communicative ability – at the disposal of the phenomenological analyst, provides him [the analyst] with a unique extension of his operating base. Now the analyst can really use the eyes of the [subject] . . . Yet he must not be under the illusion that these eyes are his own eyes. They remain at best new mirrors, and by no means undistorting mirrors (Spiegelberg, 1975, p. 51).

The new material gained in this way should not only increase the analyst's insights but also provide a better foundation for exercises in imaginative self-transposal. By combining the two techniques, analyst and subject together should be able to penetrate further into the meanings of the latter's life-world. (Such an approach is sometimes termed participant-observation.)

The only true phenomenology is firsthand phenomenology: the study of oneself through pure reflection. The methods described above are approximations of true phenomenology only. This raises a number of problems. Criteria of truth can be applied in self-study, but not in either imaginative self-transposal or co-operative encounter and exploration. Thus two phenomenologists, studying the same subject, may achieve different insights. Furthermore, neither can know which is right. (This last argument applies particularly to descriptive phenomenology – see below.) Perhaps most importantly, phenomenological investigation is dependent upon communication, upon intersubjectivity (the making of one's meanings – the interpretations placed on the elements of the life-world – available to others). Not only does this imply specific problems regarding the communicative abilities of subject and analyst but also, more generally, it raises major questions regarding the nature of the communication text, which is most commonly expressed in language. As Giddens (1979, pp. 40–41) argues:

a gulf divides the text, as a particular articulation of language, from whatever intention an author may have had in writing it.

Thus:

> To argue that texts can be illuminatingly studied as situated productions is to insist that there are connections between the two ways in which 'meaning' is ordinarily employed in English: what someone means to say, write or do, and what that which is said, written or done means.

(The difference is between intention and interpretation.) This creates problems for the procedure of bracketing, with the analyst suspending his interpretations of words:

> One of the main tasks of the study of the text, or indeed cultural products of any kind, must be precisely to examine the divergencies which can become intuited between the circumstances of their production and the meanings sustained by their subsequent escape from the horizon of their creator or creators. These meanings are never 'contained' in the text as such . . . *the consequences* of *actions chronically escape their initiators' intentions in processes of objectification* (p. 44).

Given that phenomenological methods can penetrate life-worlds and provide insight into general essences, it is then possible to pursue other aspects of phenomenology. Husserl's aims were not merely to explicate individual life-worlds. He sought to identify the nature of that which is left, absolute knowledge, after the empirical individual subject is bracketed away. (This is what Husserl called *epoché*, making 'only such judgements as do not depend for their validity on a spatio-temporal world', Baumann, 1978, p. 119.) The residue is:

> pure consciousness: consciousness which is not anybody's, consciousness free of all earthly attachments . . . [lacking] tradition, history, culturally pre-defined patterns of cognition, social practice . . . [leaving as a residue] the tough nucleus which is explicable only for itself, and not reducible any more to either tradition, culture or society (Baumann, 1978, p. 121)

It is the content of the human mind which has not been socialized, nor has it received any of the learned meanings of a milieu. Husserl's belief in the existence of such pure consciousness or absolute knowledge is represented as a belief in transcendental subjectivity – a seat of all meanings. Its discovery requires the disposal of empirical meanings and the retention of that which is given to humans a priori. Thus he presented phenomenology as a science, as a procedure (transcendental reduction) which would identify absolute truth (hence in the end two phenomenologists could not disagree) rather than provide an alternative focus on the mundane.

To Husserl, transcendental reduction would assist the solution of the problems of hermeneutic phenomenology, involving the interpretation of the meanings of the contents of pure consciousness. Initially, the field of *hermeneutics* involved the interpretation of theological texts. It is now used for the interpretation of all texts, with the goal of understanding their authors' meanings.

The term *verstehen* – interpretative understanding – is generally associated with the goals of hermeneutics. According to Outhwaite (1975), four aspects of a person may be studied: physical facts – which may signify aspects of non-physical facts (e.g. a mental state); state of mind; what he or she is doing; and why something is being done, what its motivation is. *Verstehen* is involved in the fourth of these:

> we 'understand' people's states of mind (and make inferences about their motives and intentions) with the aid of: (a) visible signs, voluntary or involuntary . . . ; (b) explicit statements . . . ; (c) a knowledge of the 'facts of the situation' which leads us to expect one sort of attitude or intention rather than another . . . [by understanding] we mean not that we know what it is to feel these emotions or the force of certain motives . . . but rather that we understand the 'situation' in which these emotions or intentions 'make sense' (Outhwaite, 1975, p. 15).

Thus hermeneutics seeks to explicate the meanings behind actions, to provide an appreciation of why a certain action was taken, rather than to explain it. It is an appreciation of context rather than an attempt at prediction.

Verstehen as a concept is associated with the philosopher Wilhem Dilthey, who differed from Husserl over the issue of pure consciousness (Rose, 1981). It is close to idealism in that it seeks to understand why people did what they did, and do what they do, in terms of their situational context. It introduces the phenomenological concept of meaning to this context – the life-world is made up of the products of intentionality, the assumptions people make about elements in their consciousness. It is achieved, according to Gadamer (see Outhwaite, 1975, p. 104 and Giddens, 1976, pp. 55–57) through *discourse*. In the study of contemporary events, this is a discourse between subject and analyst. In the study of the past:

> Understanding a text from a historical period remote from our own . . . or from a culture very different from our own is . . . essentially a creative process in which the observer, through penetrating an alien mode of existence, enriches his own self-knowledge through acquiring knowledge of others (Giddens, 1976, p. 17).

The dialogue, via texts, both enriches the analyst's understanding and enables the subject to divulge meanings; the analyst learns to live the life of the subject by participating in his language. Hermeneutics, then, is basically an empirical science, in that it seeks to explicate meanings at the phenomenal level and does not seek universal truths lying beneath those meanings.

Phenomenology was developed largely as a science of studying the individual, as a counter to certain contemporary trends in psychology. For certain social sciences, therefore, notably those involved in the study of society itself rather than the individuals who constitute it, there was a need to adapt the phenomenological perspective to their ends. Such was the task undertaken by Alfred Schutz, whose research focused on what is described in the title of his major work, explicating *The Phenomenology of the Social World* (Schutz, 1972). This was set in the general context of phenomenology, with its goal of advancing intersubjective understanding and its foundation in the subjectivity of the life-world. But Schutz argued that the everyday social world is a 'taken for granted' world, which is not normally reflected on when actions occur:

> In the world of routine, everything is taken for granted and therefore unknown . . . most routine tasks of daily life are accomplished without engaging human analytical powers . . . The world of routine . . . is not, therefore, an object of active interpretation or re-interpretation. Unless challenged, we have no 'need' to motivate routine actions to others and to ourselves (Baumann, 1978, pp. 176–177)

Given this foundation, interpretative sociology does not seek to undertake hermeneutic discourse, nor to engage in transcendental reduction. Instead, it is looking for general meanings which exist as part of the routine of daily life, in a life-world whose meanings are fixed:

> What we are thus seeking is the invariant, unique, a priori structure of the mind, in particular of a society composed of living minds (Schutz, 1972, p. 44).

The taken-for-granted world comprises a 'stock of knowledge'. Within it – and 'based upon a stock of previous experiences of it, our own experiences and those handed down to us by our parents and teachers' (Schutz, 1971, p. 208) – activity occurs. Such activity is of two types: *action* involves the intent to do something, and when completed it constitutes a performance; *conduct* is spontaneous. Both types of activity involve operating within the taken-for-granted world of implicit meanings. One reacts habitually to certain stimuli (which is not to claim, of course, that all people react in the same way, for the same stimulus may be given different meanings in different life-worlds).

Schutz's proposed methodology for the study of the phenomenology of the social world was based on his appreciation of the sociology of Max Weber, not only their shared belief in the crucial importance of subjective meanings as the controllers of action and conduct but also Weber's analytical procedures. Regarding the former, Schutz (1972, p. 6) stressed that sociology is the 'study of social behaviour by interpreting its subjective meaning as found in the intentions of individuals'. Regarding the latter, he proposed a methodology based on Weber's conception of ideal types:

> Again and again Weber refers to the problem of the ideal type as the central

problem of all the social sciences. Our studies have shown how well-founded this conception is. For the world of contemporaries and the world of predecessors can only be comprehended in an ideal-typical way (Schutz, 1972, p. 226).

Meanings can be studied in one of three ways, he argues: those expressing the intentions of a particular person in a particular context (which is the domain of history); those expressed as averages (the domain of statistics); and those expressing the intentions of an ideal-typical actor, which are the subject-matter of intepretative sociology. The only social reality that can be comprehended, given the inability to penetrate the mind of others, is that typically comprehended.

The study of ideal types is presented by Schutz as the best of several possible ways of achieving an understanding of the taken-for-granted world and of action and conduct within it. The analyst could seek to study himself in a similar situation, and project his behaviour on that of the subject, or he could study the subject's behaviour and infer both the effect of the action and its relationships to the intended effect (i.e. the motive). Schutz's preference is for a methodology in which:

> he can resort to his own knowledge of the customary behaviour of the person involved and from this deduce the latter's in-order-to and because-motives (Schutz, 1972, p. 175).

from knowledge of the type to which the subject belongs. Thus the observer identifies types within his population, individuals who have 'one and only one typical motive for a typical act' (Schutz, 1972, p. 188).

Typification is valuable for the analyst both because it circumvents some of the problems of phenomenological method and hermeneutic discourse – especially with regard to a taken-for-granted world whose essences cannot be plumbed – and also because it is a representation of how the taken-for-granted world is structured by subjects. Individuals perform typical acts because they have typified the world, and so the task of the interpretative sociologist is to identify those separate typifications. Such types are not 'formed by social scientists at random without check or restraint' (Schutz, 1964, p. 18). They must comply with four postulates: first, relevance; second, adequacy – 'each term . . . must be so constructed that a human act performed within the life-world by an individual actor in the way indicated by the typical construction would be reasonable and understandable for the actor himself as well as his fellow-man' (p. 19); third, logically consistent; and fourth, compatible – 'The system of ideal types must contain only scientifically verifiable assumptions, which have to be fully compatible with the whole of our scientific knowledge' (p. 19). Together:

> These postulates give the necessary guarantees that social sciences do in fact deal with the real social world, the one and unitary life-world of us all, and not with

a strange fancy-world independent of and without connection to this everyday life-world (p. 19).

Thus his phenomenology of the taken-for-granted world can be submitted to positivist evaluation as a true representation of action.

Related to Schutz's work is the field of *ethnomethodology*: 'Schutz supplied theoretical foundations to what ethnomethodology presented as a programme of empirical study' (Baumann, 1978, p. 188). The role of the ethnomethodologist, according to Garfinkel (1967), is to make the ways in which people conduct their daily lives accountable, i.e. 'observable and reportable'. It is, then, the study of the methodologies used by individuals to structure and carry out their daily lives. Such study is intersubjective, in that it involves understanding procedures that are common-sense to the subjects (common-sense involves subjects 'taking for granted that what is said will be made out in accordance with methods that need not be specified': Garfinkel, 1967, p. 30). Thus:

> the anticipation that persons *will* understand, the occasionality of expressions, the specific vagueness of references, the retrospective-prospective sense of a present occurrence, waiting for something later in order to see what was meant before, are sanctioned properties of common discourse (Garfinkel, 1967, p. 41).

Ethnomethodologists study the contents of that common discourse (such as conversations) in order to identify the methodologies of taken-for-granted worlds. They are not academic voyeurs, acting randomly. They aim, like other social scientists who base their research on phenomenology, to get below what Baumann (1978, p. 189) calls 'the technology of life', to identify its basic meanings, even if they cannot comprehend how these meanings are produced. Thus:

> Phenomena best serve the purposes of ethnomethodological empirical activity if reduced to window-panes through which one could look directly to the intricate clock work which they hide rather than disclose in daily life. But then the ethnomethodologist would not be interested in specific, non-universal and contingent shapes of cog-wheels and catches which made the phenomena as they are: he would try instead to model the 'general', indispensable properties of the clockwork purified as much as possible of all specific content . . . ethnomethodological research is not *of* phenomena, but *through* phenomena (Baumann, 1978, pp. 189–190).

It is in this sense that ethnomethodology is rooted in phenomenology.

These approaches have several elements in common, therefore, as social science philosophies and methodologies. Giddens (1976, pp. 52–53) draws the following four conclusions with regard to interpretative sociologies: first, they stress that *verstehen* is not only a scientific goal but also a basic feature of social life – understanding is the foundation of action and conduct; second, analysts draw on the same resources as their subjects – the former in 'scientific theorizing' and the latter in 'practical theorizing'; third, much knowledge of the social world is taken for granted by the subjects and cannot easily be expressed, especially in the format of positivist science; and fourth, social scientific concepts must be linked to 'those used by laymen in sustaining a meaningful social world' (p. 53). Despite links with positivism, therefore, the interpretative sociologies, starting from their bases in phenomenology and hermeneutics, present a view of the world as it is perceived by the subjects and not as it is structured a priori by the observers.

Existentialism

Like most of the other philosophies discussed in this chapter, existentialism is not a unified school of thought. Rather it is a grouping of writers whose works, according to one commentator, might lead a 'bewildered outsider' to conclude 'that the only thing they have in common is a marked aversion to each other' (Kaufmann, 1975, p. 11). The best-known existentialist is the French philosopher Jean-Paul Sartre; Jaspers and Heidegger are included as existentialists by many, as are Kierkegaard, Nietzsche and Dostoevsky. Their existentialism, according to Kaufmann, is 'a label for several widely different revolts against traditional philosophy' (p. 11) displaying 'passionate concern with questions that arise from life, the moral pathos and the firm belief that . . . philosophy has to be lived' (p. 51).

Two key phrases are often used to characterize the tenets of existentialism: 'man makes himself' and 'existence before essence'. Unlike phenomenologists, therefore, existentialists – especially atheistic existentialists such as Sartre and Heidegger – do not believe in general essences, pure consciousness, and ultimate knowledge. Reality is created by the free acts of human agents, for and by themselves:

> The self that existentialism seeks is each person's individual self, which he must forge for himself out of such senseless circumstances, such meaningless limitations, as are given him. This self-creation – the making of one's essence from mere existence – is demanded of each of us because . . . there is no *single* essence of humanity (Grene, 1959, p. 41).

This lack of a single essence, Grene argues, reflects the atheism of Sartre and others: it is based on the axiom that 'No God, therefore no essence of man' (p. 44), which forces the conclusion that human values can only be derived from human exsitence.

The nature of those values is brought out in the relationships between the individual and, first, the world of things and, secondly, the world of others. With regard to the former, realization of individual freedom produces dread, because of:

the appalling consciousness that I, and I alone, have, absurdly and without reason, brought order out of chaos; alone, crudely and stupidly . . . have made a world out of nothing: and with that awareness my world itself totters on the brink of the helplessness from which I come . . . It is dread before emptiness – before annihilation – before nothing (Grene, 1959, p. 52).

With regard to others, any revelation of these produces 'annihilation of myself as subject . . . [which] I am bound to try by every means in my power to overcome' (Grene, 1949, p. 79). Further, this revelation of myself to others creates fear and shame because:

> instead of being engaged as a free agent in a project of my own, I am . . . an object in his view . . . I am what *he* makes of me, not what I make myself . . . Fear and shame are the two proper and immediate reactions to the intrusion of another person into my world (Grene, 1959, pp. 80–81).

The only counter to shame and fear is aggression, to threaten the observer with extinction so that one can become a free agent again.

Existentialism postulates atomistic individualism, therefore, which leads to certain attitudes towards the physical world and to others in it. The purpose of existentialism, as practised by Sartre and others, has been to explore these attitudes, particularly their absurd and tragic characteristics. Their explanations have largely involved using fiction to depict these attitudes and characteristics, rather than through any formal methodology. The purpose is to demonstrate how man creates his world, in a context where the only constraints are others doing likewise.

The significance of existentialism, according to Olafson (1967), is in its protest against many elements of modern society. It has sought to heighten self-consciousness and to indicate to individuals that they are 'autonomous moral agents, capable of raising and resolving for themselves all questions about what they are to do' (p. 238). It stresses freedom, decision, and responsibility: 'it is through free and responsible decisions that man becomes authentically himself' (Macquarrie, 1972, p. 4). Other basic theories are finitude, guilt, alienation, despair and death, many of which reflect the frustrations man experiences in his attempts to create an authentic self and which lead to existentialism being a dominantly pessimistic philosophy. 'They become truly themselves only to the extent that they freely choose themselves' (p. 161) but being part of a society, part of a crowd, hampers choice and generates despair and alienation. If choice is hampered then man becomes inauthentic and drifts along at the mercy of events rather than creating a personal future. Societies, like individuals, can experience inauthentic histories. As individuals lose control of their destinies in modern advanced technological societies dominated by large corporations and the state, so alienation increases. Existentialism proclaims this alienation and seeks to replace it by a society in which human dignity is enhanced, and to that extent it is a critique, both political and, to some, theological.

According to Macquarrie (1972, p. 8), 'Most existentialists are phenomenologists, though there are many phenomenologists who are not existentialists'. The agreement comes about with regard to such concepts as intentionality, but phenomenology goes further than individual intentions with its search for essences and universal structures, and the consequent lack of attention to personal idiosyncrasies. Existentialists are not concerned with essential phenomenology (p. 57); they accept some of the phenomenological method but stay at the level of existence for their analyses. Their methodology is one of drawing the individual out from the crowd, from the pressures to conform in society, and to advance the self. This promotes individualism. In existentialist psychiatry (practised by R.D. Laing, *inter alia*) the aim is to create authentic beings, for example, whereas existentialist education involves the teacher opening up opportunities for the student, but never leading the way in. In literature, as indicated above, existentialist writers have emphasized tragedy, despair and absurdity:

> reminding us that techniques alone cannot solve the human problem, for this is finally an existential problem. They are not so much pessimists as realists who know that there are no utopian solutions to the pathos of existence (Macquarrie, 1972, p. 211).

In ethics, existentialists stress being 'true to oneself' rather than conforming to a law imposed by society which reflects past custom, ensures stability, but promotes human stagnation. And in theology, too, it stresses the moral nature of the authentic individual. To some, 'existentialism implies atheistic humanism, but to others it can lead to 'those very limits of existence where faith arises' (Macquarrie, 1972, p. 267) without providing any proof of the existence of a God.

Existentialism has many similarities with original Marxism (see p. 92) in its concern with the alienation of man in society. It differs, however, in its solution to the problems of inauthentic existence (although again there are common elements between aspects of existentialism and anarchist-Marxism). Its aim is the realization of self and its methodology is to use whatever means are relevant (psychiatric analysis, education, literature, visual art) to illustrate personal inauthenticity to man. It has elements of individualism. It stresses that man must learn to live in a society with others, however, but argues that one begins with the individual, not with society, in order to create a more human existence than is experienced at present.

Humanistic approaches in human geography

A common feature of the approaches discussed in this chapter is their focus on subjectivity. To idealists, to phenomenologists, and to existentialists knowledge of the world does not exist independent of the knower. Instead, it exists only in man's experience of the world, and can only be appreciated by sensitive analysis of that experience. Man's behaviour cannot be explained in the positivist sense, therefore, but only appreciated, and the ontology is one of being not of existence. On this definition, a humanistic geography is one which studies man in the world that he creates as a thinking being. It aims at *verstehen*, at an understanding of man in his environment. (Note that whereas most humanistic approaches are phrased at the level of the individual, Jackson (1981) has argued that phenomenology can be used to provide insights at the societal level. See also Relph, 1981b.)

The need for a 'subjective' approach in human geography has long been recognized and advanced: Sauer wrote of the phenomenology of landscape, in 1925, for example; eleven years later, Wooldridge (1936) claimed that historical geography must seek to view the countryside through the eyes of the farmer; Ralph Brown's (1943) classic historical geography of the American Eastern Seaboard in 1810 presented it through the eyes of a mythical inhabitant, Thomas Keystone; and in 1947 John Wright introduced the term *geosophy* as part of his contention that geographical knowledge is part of the mental stock of all humans:

> geographical knowledge of one kind or another is universal among men . . . nearly every important activity in which man engages . . . is to some extent affected by the geographical knowledge at his disposal (Wright, 1947, pp. 13–14).

But these were relatively isolated statements which had little impact on the profession at large: the case for a humanistic geography has only been argued forcibly since about 1960.

Advocacy of humanistic perspectives has taken two forms in the geographical literature. In the first, a general humanistic (or subjectivist) orientation is proposed, usually without reference to any one of the philosophies outlined above; in a few cases, the advocacy is for some combination of elements from two or more of those approaches. The second type consists of arguments for one of the three: idealism, phenomenology, and existentialism. (Much of the advocacy has been as much anti-positivistic as prohumanistic, see Jackson, 1981; the latter elements are concentrated on here.) The two types of argument are considered separately.

General humanistic perspectives
One of the first geographers to attract a wide audience with his advocacy of a humanistic approach was Kirk. His position was initially developed in 1951, but most authors refer to a later, revised and more accessible statement (Kirk, 1951, 1963, 1979). He separated what he termed the 'geographical environment' into two components: the phenomenal environment and the behavioural environment. The latter comprises those 'facts of the

Phenomenal Environment ... perceived by human beings with motives, preferences, modes of thinking, and traditions drawn from their social, cultural context' (Kirk, 1963, p. 366); only facts in the behavioural environment are relevant to the study of decision-making. Somewhat similar arguments were put forward by Lowenthal (1961). He argued for the study of what he called 'personal geographies': unique milieux containing information which is 'inspired, edited, and distorted by feeling' (p. 257). Lowenthal put greater stress on the interpretations of the elements in such behavioural environments than did Kirk.

In neither of these papers was there any explicit reference to the humanistic philosophies (Lowenthal refers to a large volume of material on the psychology of perception, however, which may in part explain why some human geographers equate humanistic approaches with the study of perception). It was only in the 1970s that full reference to these philosophies was made. Thus Tuan (1976, p. 266), for example, argues for a humanistic geography which:

> achieves an understanding of the human world by studying people's relations with nature, their geographical behavior as well as their feelings and ideas in regard to space and place.

and for:

> the study of a people's spatial feelings and ideas in the stream of experience (Tuan, 1974, p. 213).

Such a geography would focus on space and place as they enter human experience, and would enable people to probe their personal geographies more deeply. The utility of such an approach is expressed by Buttimer (1979, p. 30):

> The overall task of geography has often been cited in terms as broad as the drama of human life within its total environmental setting. If the goals of human existence are seen to be the fulfillment of human potential, then state of *becoming* should be more important than *state of being*. If such human becoming can be construed as part of total becoming within the biosphere, then our time-worn geographic perspective may in fact be one of the most valuable contributions possible towards the resolution of social and ecological issues.

A humanistic (clearly in Buttimer's case very much an existentialist) perspective in geography, it is claimed, will enable man to know himself better and so improve the quality of his existence. Thus:

> a principal aim of modern humanism in geography is the reconciliation of social science and man, to accommodate understanding and wisdom, objectivity and subjectivity, and materialism and idealism (Ley and Samuels, 1978, p. 9).

And:

Humanism is the conviction that men and women can best improve the circumstances of their lives by thinking and acting for themselves, and especially by exercising their capacity for reason (Relph, 1981a, p. 7).

Advocacy for particular humanistic approaches
Apart from the general advocacy outlined above, each of the particular humanistic approaches discussed earlier in this chapter has been presented to human geographers (and by human geographers) as a viable philosophy for the discipline; some have been stressed more than others, with phenomenology the most popular. Again, as with the general advocacies, the case presented has been as much against positivism as pro. . . . The aim has been to convert geographers to an alternative perspective because of the failures that were currently espoused (whether positivist or structuralist).

The case for *idealism* has been argued most strongly by two historical geographers who were influenced by Collingwood's (1947) *The Idea of History*. Harris (1971) was especially impressed by the argument that historiography is a synthetic practice bringing together, by the perceptive interpretations of documents and other texts, material so that:

> Although a complete understanding of complex particular situations may be impossible, synthesis does attempt to find a coherent path through the endlessly complex welter of interrelated facts that lie behind them, and to offer an explanation that is plausible and full (p. 164).

Such a synthesis is achieved by 'an idealist interpretation of explanation in history . . . a historian comes to understand an event as he rethinks the thought lying behind it' (p. 165), Harris argues that a similar approach could be used by geographers:

> to understand a particular region, place, or landscape, or to treat a theme . . . bearing on the character of a particular place, is to achieve a synthesizing understanding analogous to that in history. A geographer may have to understand the thought . . . lying behind a great many human actions; . . . he may have to deal with human actions which were not the result of conscious thought, and be able to handle generalizations from social science (p. 168).

In another piece, Harris (1978) presents his appreciation of what he calls 'the historical mind' – representing the idealist conception of historiography – and arguing, in the footsteps of Carl Sauer, Andrew Clark and others, for the development of a parallel geographic imagination which would involve each researcher immersing himself in a 'region' just as a historian does with a 'period': the result would be 'a more penetrating understanding of an intricate part of the world, an appreciation of the complexity of human experience, and much pleasure' (p. 126).

To Guelke (1974), the axiomatic feature of an idealist approach in human geography is that the discipline is concerned with 'the rational actions and products of human minds' (p. 193). Action implies intentions and intentions involve the application of theories. Thus:

> The intention behind an action can be regarded as the source of its power, and the theory in it can be considered to be the guidance system (p. 197).

The theory is that held by the actor: it is his view of the world, modified by the data which he receives. Thus to understand actions:

> The human geographer simply attempts to reconstruct the thought behind the actions that were taken. He does not need theories of his own, because he is concerned with the theories expressed in the actions of the individual being investigated (p. 198).

Initially, Guelke (1975, 1982) argued for the value of the idealist approach in historical geography. He later extended his case to urban geography (Guelke, 1978) and, by implication, to all human geography.

The case for *phenomenology* has been made by a number of authors. (Some of them amalgamated phenomenology and idealism, see Billinge, 1977, p. 56; Guelke (1978, p. 54) counters this, however, arguing that phenomenologists, in their concern for emotions and meanings, do 'not give us the tools to understand or explain human behaviour in an intersubjective or objective way . . . The idealist shares the phenomenologist's concern with understanding the different meanings people attach to their surroundings, but at an intellectual rather than an emotional level'.) Relph (1970), for example, provides a brief outline of the nature of phenomenology and notes that some of its concepts have been implicitly incorporated into geographical works (such as Lowenthal, 1961). Fuller development of this approach, he argues, is valuable because:

> Man and the world . . . constitute a unity through their mutual implication, though it is man's intentionality that gives meaning to the world and it is only through an examination of these intentions that we can attempt to comprehend this unity (p. 197).

(See also Relph, 1981a.)

A more detailed evaluation was provided by Mercer and Powell (1972), who reviewed not only the phenomenology of Husserl but also the developments within sociology represented by the works of Schutz and Garfinkel (see p. 62). They discuss the 'points of sympathy' linking phenomenology with idealism but argue with regard to the latter 'that Collingwood's theory of historical explanation underplays the great force of emotional and self-conscious motivation behind much human action' (p. 34; see also Gibson's 1978, critique of idealism). Note that Guelke (1976, p. 169) argues against geographers asking not only what people thought but why they thought it: such investigations 'fall within the domain of the medical and psychological sciences' and are 'clearly outside the scope of human geography conceived as a study of man's activities on the land'. With regard to human geography, Mercer and Powell (1972) conclude, in antipositivist vein, that there is a need for 'a viewpoint which emphasizes the richness of man's experience and his perceptions of the world' (p. 51). Behavioural work (see p. 37), they claim, only goes partway towards this goal, because 'it is deeply permeated by positivistic ideas at all levels'. (See also Cox, 1981; Ley, 1981.)

Of the various phenomenological approaches, those relating to the sociology of the everyday world, to ethnomethodology, and to hermeneutics have received little attention from geographers, even in the form of programmatic statements only. With regard to the first two, Ley (1977) has criticized contemporary social and behavioural geography for its positivistic psychologism and investigated whether phenomenology offers 'an underpinning to a reinvigorated social geography concerned with group action which culminates in a landscape effect'. He argues that Schutz's work provides:

> a pertinent framework and underpinning for a social geography which examines the social and cognitive contexts antecedent to a spatial fact (p. 507).

because of the important role of place in group and individual action. A social geography of the taken-for-granted world would focus on the meaning of places as created by the intentions of human groups. Smith (1981), too, argues for a methodology based on Schutz's work, allied to a philosophy which admits exploratory hypotheses, generalizations, and explanatory theory. (She excludes 'philosophies adhering to the tenet that inner truth may be divined by reason and trained intuition, for these dispense with the primacy of observational method' p. 293.) Material is gathered through participant observation, by reflection upon and selection from observations and experiences gained 'transactionally' (i.e. through contact with subjects and participation in the activities in their taken-for-granted worlds). Out of this come analytical constructs, understandings of behaviour obtained empathetically, and from them it is possible to move towards generalizations based on 'comparative analysis of the ostensibly unique' (p. 297).

Regarding *hermeneutics*, Rose (1981) has pointed out the relevance of Dilthey's arguments to a human geography:

> If we accept the premises that: (1) human geography takes place entirely within a sphere of signs, (2) that some of these signs are found together in texts either spoken, written, gestured or acted out, and (3) it is the job of human geographers to interpret such texts as a spectator in order to make certain statements about actors operating within the texts, and further (4) to communicate the meanings of such phenomena as he should deem important

back to the actors involved . . . what is required of geographers . . . is not to obtain directly the meanings to which the texts refer but rather the attempt to rediscover those meanings from the text, from the transmitted tradition in the text and from their own worlds. (p. 124)

Such a dialogical project has been undertaken by Buttimer (1981) into the history of geography. She also uses the hermeneutic perspective in arguing for applied geography:

> awakening responsibility among various sectors of society. Does this role of provocateur, of facilitator of such a movement, not require that we eventually allow the 'objects' of our research to become 'subjects' of their own individual and collective lives? We may have expertise to offer . . . but to imagine that we can write the script, set the stage, and manage the production, seems not only pretentious, but could also be destructive of . . . creativity (Buttimer, 1979, p, 33).

An *existentialist* approach to human geography has been argued by Samuels (1978, 1981). Man, he claims, defines himself spatially. Part of his creation of an identity, his confirmation of himself, involves his relationship with the environment. What were objects prior to this process become places:

> a world in which all objects are equally important is anarchical . . . partial space is the assignment of meanings to places and systems of places (Samuels, 1978, p. 32).

Man originates in an alienated condition. His creation of places provides him with roots, so that a landscape is a biography of that creation, a statement of the 'existential origins of spatial arrangements, relations and attachments' (Samuels, 1981, p. 126). Some landscapes are individual, and are the biographies of their creators, but there are general landscapes too, reflecting the experiences of human groups in shared situations, such as the geography of post-Second World War American cities. An existential geography, according to Samuels, would seek to understand those shared contexts:

> Effectively, an 'existential geography' is a type of historical geography that endeavours to reconstruct a landscape in the eyes of its occupants, users, explorers and students in the light of historical situations that condition, modify, or change relationships (Samuels, 1981, p. 129).

It is the ability to use existentialist methods to reconstruct societal as well as individual spatial biographies that leads Jackson (1981, p. 303) to argue that 'existential phenomenology [is] more important for social science than either philosophy alone': it allows 'an analysis of the spatial structure of social relations'.

Humanistic geography

In the chapter on positivist approaches in human geography, a large literature was discussed relating to both the methodology of positivism and the products of its applications. The nature of positivistic human geography was indicated by its output. Such an approach is not possible for the present chapter, largely because the output is much smaller. As Relph (1981b) wrote, presumably in about 1979:

> In the numerous geographical periodicals and books published since 1970 there are, to my knowledge, just nine papers which deal explicitly with the relations between geography and phenomenology and six books which use phenomenological approaches to examine geographical phenomena (p. 106).

The numbers are larger now, especially with regard to substantive works, but Harris's (1978, p. 134) statement that:

> In North America at present, those who call themselves 'humanist geographers' are inclined to philosophical reading and methodological writing . . . whereas cultural and historical geographers tend to pursue their old ways no more affected by the new humanism than by the spatial analysis of the 1960s.

still holds true (although 'programmatic' may be a better adjective than 'methodological' with which to describe the writings). To a considerable extent, therefore, there is relatively little to review to illustrate the nature of humanistic work.

One reason why there is so little to review may be that the programmatic statements have had little effect (note that Relph, 1981b, points out that the language of phenomenology is 'exceedingly difficult to penetrate', p. 102, and that 'without doing phenomenology, it may be impossible to understand it', p. 106), or that the advocacy has been in some ways incomplete. Billinge (1977), for example, writes of the attempts to incorporate a phenomenological approach into human geography as 'witness to a fundamental misconception of the purist nature of phenomenology – at best a misnomer; at worst yet more evidence of the disturbing tendency to adopt terminology the exact meaning of which is manifestly misunderstood' (p. 64; see also Agnew and Duncan, 1981). He concludes that 'phenomenological we have by no means become' (p. 67). More strongly, Entrikin argues that this is because a humanistic approach to replace the positivist is impossible:

> humanist geography does not offer a viable alternative to, nor a presuppositionless basis for, scientific geography . . . Rather, the humanist approach is best understood as a form of criticism (Entrikin, 1976, p. 616).

In part, he claims, this is because the humanist approach is 'methodologically obscure'; the goals of understanding man's meaningful experiences seem to lead to a situation in which 'any method is acceptable'

(p. 629). There is, indeed, relatively little discussion of method in the philosophical literature, let alone the geographical. (Billinge, 1977, p. 63, writes that 'phenomenology has not, in general, concerned itself with the details of implementation, but with broader aspects of conception and cogitation. It is not a "practical" philosophy'.) Many writers suggest that humanistic work involves thinking rather than practical activity, plus communication, either with the texts or with actors. Thus to Ley and Samuels (1978, p. 14):

> While humanistic methodology is eclectic and the sources for interpretation are numerous, ranging from archival research to participant observation, for the geographer the methods converge upon a group in place and the landscape they occupy.

Doing humanistic research is very largely a personal matter, therefore, involving intuition and imaginative interpretation. It differs from the behaviourist work discussed in the previous chapter in that whereas such work focuses on behaviour, which is observable and quantifiable, humanistic work focuses on experience, which is neither. Participant observation, or experiential field work, is possible for contemporary research into the 'taken-for-granted' world (Rowles, 1978). Nevertheless:

> It is certainly questionable whether any two phenomenologists can ever have exactly the same 'intuitions' of the same phenomenon, or indeed know whether or not they have the same intuitions. It is not possible to *prove* anything by the phenomenological method, and . . . *argument* is impossible (Mercer and Powell, 1972, p. 14).

For such reasons, Entrikin (1976) argued that the eclectic work in humanistic geography provided at best only a form of criticism of positivist work:

> As criticism it provides a potentially useful function in reaffirming the importance of the study of meaning and value in human geography, making geographers aware of their often extreme interpretations of science, and making scientists aware of the social and cultural factors involved in so-called objective research (p. 632).

Despite these reservations, various authors note that much work has been done in human geography which adopts the essentially subjectivist stance of the humanistic approaches even if it does not proceed very far with them – to the identification, for example, of pure consciousness. Much of this work has been done in cultural and social geography, in particular historical geography. The forms of economic geography discussed in the previous chapters have been little affected, despite claims that they could be (Guelke, 1978; Wallace, 1978). Thus in reviewing the literature, the emphasis must be on applications to certain aspects of human geography only. As already stressed, most of these applications are humanistic but have not fully embraced the philosophy and methodology of any of the three approaches outlined earlier. Their general orientation is outlined here, without any discussion of the relative absence of philosophical guidelines.

Historical geography The reconstruction of spatial distributions and patterns of land-use in the past has long been a popular component of human geography, presented by some as an end in itself and by others as an aid in understanding the present. Among historical geographers, there have been debates regarding the best methodology, whether to study cross-sections through time or changes over time, for example, but data availability has been a severe limitation on the questions that can sensibly be asked. In summarising the preoccupations of historical geographers, however, Prince (1971) was able to identify 'three arbitrarily defined, if not truly separate, realms of knowledge' (p. 4):

1 The features of the landscape and human society in the past, which are verifiable by evidence and so form 'real worlds of the past'.
2 The images of the world held by residents of the past, as influences on their actions, creating 'imagined worlds of the past'.
3 Reconstructions of past worlds in terms of later models, providing 'abstract worlds of the past'.

The exact nature of these three realms may now be questioned – see the discussion of realism in the next chapter (pp. 101–103) – but the typification is of particular value here in highlighting the second realm, the behavioural environments of the past.

In the longest section of his essay, on 'imagined worlds of the past', Prince notes that once the question 'Why?' is asked regarding the real worlds:

> the full answer can no longer be sought in the external world, because motives, attitudes, preferences and prejudices must be examined as well as works and deeds (p. 24).

The ways in which historical geographers seek to answer that question depend, as Prince illustrates, on the evidence available to them. His bibliography indicates the volume of such work, on a wide variety of themes, times, and places.

In terms of the humanistic approaches discussed here, the basic thrust of much of this historical geography has been idealist; the researchers have sought to reproduce the actions of individuals and groups by identifying their theoretical bases. This is illustrated by work on the settlement of the New World where, as Heathcote (1965) and Powell (1970) show for Australia, there was a conflict between two theories, or appraisals, of the environment: the official and the popular. Such studies are almost entirely particularistic, emphasizing the unique, if not singular, aspects of the subject matter, whether theories of the physical or of the social environment (Powell, 1971). Powell (1977) has sought to generalize such enterprises into a framework termed eiconics – the study of images, which are communicated in the settlement process – but although he concludes that:

> Our journey through the changing geography of the New World illustrates sufficiently well that its landscapes have always mirrored the ideas and ideals of its inhabitants (p. 174).

this does not lead him beyond the idealist conception of historical geography to the sorts of generalizations about essences that characterize phenomenology.

As indicated earlier, an existentialist approach to geography sees landscape as the biography of its creator: 'The landscape is thoroughly and permanently imbued with struggle, tension, and dialectical conflict' (Samuels, 1978b, p. 293). This theme is illustrated by Samuels with regard to the landscape changes in China stimulated by Mao's 'cosmic battle between man and nature' (p. 294). His general thesis is that 'the created landscapes of men are . . . contingent upon contexts, but the responsibility of authors' (Samuels, 1979, p. 64). Most landscapes are created by key individuals, so landscape biographies can be discerned from the geographies of their authors, whether Mao or Robert Moses (Caro, 1975). Where the authors are not identifiable individuals, then one is looking at the product of a society:

> Our human landscape is our unwitting autobiography, and all our cultural warts and blemishes, our ordinary day-to-day qualities, are there for anybody who knows how to look for them (Lewis, 1979, p. 13).

Thus:

> The man-made landscape – the ordinary run-of-the-mill things that humans have created and put upon the earth – provides strong evidence of the kind of people we are, and were, and are in process of becoming (p. 15).

so that the landscape is the text (see also Rose, 1980):

> The English landscape itself, to those who know how to read it aright, is the richest historical record we possess (Hoskins, 1955, p. 14).

Although not presented as existentialist, some other work on landscapes also presents them as biographical reflections of past society, and argues that preservation of such landscapes aids human identity. In his essay on the American landscape, for example, Lowenthal (1975a, p. 8) argues that 'simply to know that structures are durable may give residents a sense of being rooted in a place' and illustrates the use of landscape features to create a collective memory of 'a long and glorious past'. He later points out that 'The past we know about is not . . . a present that was ever experienced' (p. 25) so that:

> we shape landscapes and artifacts to conform with illusory histories, public and private, that gratify our tastes (p. 36).

Whilst the existentialist uses the landscape to provide information about earlier societies, therefore, Lowenthal claims that society recreates landscapes to present its vision of the past. This shows a disregard for history, he claims (Lowenthal, 1975b). It also writes a new chapter in the biography and illustrates the nature of a society characterized by that disregard.

The sense of place One of the areas of research that comes closest to the aims of intuitive phenomenology and its quest for elements of pure consciousness is that concerned with the links between people, individually and as groups, and places. (It should be noted that most of this work represents geography with implicit phenomenological content rather than explicit attempts to 'do phenomenological research'.) This was identified by Tuan (1976) as one of the main themes of a humanistic geography, the translation of 'mere space [into] . . . an intensely human place' (p. 269). He presented such a process as one example of the more general concept of topophilia, which embraces 'all of the human being's active ties with the material environment' (Tuan, 1974b, p. 93). Much of his work has explored themes related to this general concept (e.g Tuan, 1977).

According to one humanist geographer, the sense of place is a fundamental element in the 'taken-for-granted' world. His work is predicated on the axiom that:

> places are indeed a fundamental aspect of most existence in the world, . . . they are sources of security and identity for individuals and for groups of people

Which is followed by the statement:

> it is important that the means of experiencing, creating and maintaining significant places are not lost. Moreover there are many signs that these very means are disappearing and that 'placelessness' – the weakening of distinct and diverse experiences of places – is now a dominant force (Relph, 1976, p. 6).

(There may be something of a paradox here: if sense of place is an element of 'pure consciousness' – note that Relph does not claim this – then can it be replaced by a rootlessness created by a changing society?) Relph clearly believes that a sense of place can be created, or at least facilitated, by landscape planning (or perhaps by a lack of it) to replace the inauthenticity of the landscapes of industrial and late capitalism, by:

> allowing scope for individuals and groups to make their own places, and to give those places authenticity and significance by modifying them and by dwelling in them (p. 146).

There are strong links between such work, with its clear base in the humanistic approaches, and writing on landscape design and 'mental maps' in the behaviourist/positivist mould discussed in the previous chapter. This drew its inspiration from works such as that of the landscape architect Kevin Lynch (1960) in *The Image of the City* and on the creation of images (see Downs and Stea, 1977). Whereas such behaviourist investigations obtained their data from questionnaires and similar surveys, and manipulated these statistically, however, humanistic approaches have focused on texts and a presuppositionless approach. The nature of the texts varies widely. As already illustrated here, the landscape itself has been used by some as the repository of human meaning (see also Hugill, 1975). Literature, too, has been used as 'a perspective for how people experience their world' (Tuan, 1978, p. 194). It can provide three forms of aid to the humanist geographer, according to Tuan: it is a thought experiment revealing modes of human experience; it is an artifact, illustrating the cultural perceptions of an environment; and it is a model of geographical synthesis and writing. According to Pocock (1981a, p. 346) 'it is of the essence of literature to reveal the universal while apparently concerned with the particular': literature is the work (as are all works of art) of artists with particular 'perceptive insight' (Pocock, 1981b, p. 15) regarding contemporary situations.

Sense of place is often interpreted to cover the affective ties between individuals/groups and their (native or adopted) home areas, including their housing; see Duncan (1981). However, it is not only such home areas that are given meanings. For most people, considerable areas of space must be structured to form a life-world, for 'Space is an essential framework to all modes of thought' (Sack, 1980b, p. 4). In a review of the various conceptions of space in social thought, Sack has categorized modes of thought in a two-dimensional framework: the first dimension is a subjective/objective continuum (relating to both subject matter and method of analysis); the other is a space/substance dimension – at one pole the focus is on spatial form alone and at the other on phenomena studied in an aspatial context. He then identifies two dominant modes of thought within this framework:

1 Sophisticated-fragmented modes are characteristic of the arts, social sciences and physical sciences, in that they abstract phenomena from their context, use symbols to represent them (e.g. maps, Blakemore, 1981), and look at parts only rather than wholes.

2 Unsophisticated-fused modes are neither abstract nor based on the use of symbols; nor are they specialized.

The former are not necessarily either positivist or behaviouralist. Sack discusses the analysis of dreams and works of art, although he concludes that:

> Whether there can or cannot be ... a science [of subjective conceptions of space] is a point we will not engage ... [but] to abandon the attempt without offering an alternative mode of understanding human behaviour is to despair of knowing (Sack, 1980b, p. 116).

With respect to the unsophisticated-fused modes, he analyses the child's view of space, the normal practical view of the adult, and space as it is presented in myth and magic, and then proceeds to an investigation of the mixture of the various modes within different societies. Such work clearly has strong humanistic foundations although, as with much of the work discussed in this section, those foundations are seldom explicit. The goal is clear, however:

> Since our actions on the earth spring from our views of the world, an analysis of the meanings of geographic space in modes of thought will better enable us to explain actual behaviour in space (Sack, 1980a, p. 314).

A positivist goal, it seems, is being wedded (at least in part) to humanistic methods.

Associated with the concept of the sense of place and with the structuring of space by individuals and groups is the notion of *territoriality*. This is usually interpreted in much the same way as sense of place – 'the theory that animals, persons and groups identify with and defend territories of various spatial extents' (Seamon, 1979, p. 69) – but to some it implies considerably more. (As such, it could be considered an example of deep structure, as discussed in the section on 'structure as construct' in the next chapter, see pages 88–91.) For geographers, as for many other social scientists, appreciation of territoriality among mammals came with Ardrey's (1969) popularization of ethological work in *The Territorial Imperative*, and a cognate presentation by Morris (1967). According to Ardrey:

> The concept of territory as a genetically determined form of behaviour in many species is today accepted beyond question in the biological sciences (p. 13).

Men, too, map out territories, around themselves as individuals, around their homes, and around their nations, for example. Do they do this because they choose to or, as animals, because they must? (Is territoriality an element of pure consciousness, or a deep structure, as discussed in the next chapter?) He concludes that the latter is the case:

> We act as we do for reasons of our evolutionary past, not our cultural present . . . The dog barking at you from behind his master's fence acts for a motive indistinguishable from that of his master when the fence was built (p. 16).

Most of the geographical use of the concept of territoriality has been based on a general analogy with animal behaviour rather than as the outcome of phenomenological research. (Though see Tuan, 1976, on crowding.) Thus the practice of social distancing at the individual and neighbourhood scales, as well as at the national (with its related concept of xenophobia) has been treated as learned behaviour associated with the class conflict endemic in most societies (Johnston, 1980a, 1982a).

Man, nature and landscape The interrelationships between societies and their habitats have always been a source of interest for scholars, as Glacken's (1967) magisterial survey shows. Such a theme has obvious interest for humanistic geographers although it, like so much else, has also been subjected to positivist approaches, as in the search for techniques that will allow generalizations about landscape quality, evaluation, and preferences (Penning-Rowsell, 1981).

For humanist geographers, the study of meaning in landscapes in not something which is susceptible to positivistic analyses, although it is possible, according to Appleton (1975, p. vii), to state hypotheses and develop theories. Appleton bases his work on landscape:

> on the assumption that our aesthetic reactions to it are in part inborn, and that they can only be brought into operation if we provide them with sign-symbols of a kind which can be spontaneously apprehended by a mechanism attuned to the natural environment . . . an observer must seek to recreate something of that primitive relationship which links a creature with its habitat (Appleton, 1975, p. viii).

(Thus Appleton assumes, or hypothesises, that pure consciousness contains certain elements rather than seeking those elements in a presuppositionless way.) Appleton's search for this inborn aesthetic sense begins in animal ethology, from which he derives the main postulate of habitat theory, that animals react to their environments according to their basic needs. For an animal in a habitat he identifies four main activities – hunting, escaping, shelter-seeking, and exploring – from which he derives two primitives – seeing and hiding. The environment must provide for these, producing what he terms a prospect-refuge theory, which provides 'a frame of reference for examining the aesthetic properties of landscape' (p. 79), which he makes clear is not the only frame available. (For an alternative, focused on amenity, see Lowenthal and Prince, 1964.) The remainder of his book illustrates Appleton's belief in the viability of this theory, in a wide-ranging survey. Part of the same theme has been investigated by Tuan (1979).

The everyday world The applications of humanistic approaches to studies of people in their daily life-worlds are few. One exception is the work of Seamon (1979), who used phenomenology to explore three themes: movement, rest and encounter. Movement related to day-to-day environment dealings; rest to person-place attachments; and encounter to observation of the world (p. 17). His methodology involved the use of 'environmental experience groups' (akin to the workshops suggested by Spiegelberg, 1975, and involving co-operative encounter and exploration) which comprised people coming together and sharing their environmental experiences. Seamon recorded, transcribed and discussed the proceedings, and identified his three themes from this procedure. Together, he claims, the three constitute a *place ballet*. This involves:

> Body ballet . . . a set of integrated gestures and movements which sustain a particular task or aim (p. 54).

Combined with:

> a time-space routine . . . a set of habitual bodily behaviours which extend through a considerable portion of time (p. 55).

So that:

> Body ballets and time-space routines mix in a supportive physical environment to create place ballet – an interaction of many time-space routines and body ballets rooted in space (p. 56).

Appreciation of the centrality of this integration can lead to a humanistic application, in a dialogue between those who wish to plan places and those who live in them:

> Insiders come to discover one taken-for-granted component of the place in which they live. They recognise through their own experience the value of place ballets; they feel a wish to sustain existing place ballets and foster new ones. At the same time, outsiders recognise the ballets of places under their jurisdiction; they initiate plans and policies to protect place ballets and integrate their dynamics into larger environmental wholes (p. 152)

Whereas Seamon's work on the everyday world was based largely on Husserlian phenomenology (with no references to Schutz, for example), Ley's (1974) study of the everyday world of inner city Philadelphia integrates an idealist view (the interplay of two images: one external to the inner city, the other internal) with that of transactional sociology, arguing that:

In such a social world it is the daily verbal communication which reinforces the world's reality, and indeed molds the appearance of the environment (p. 47).

Through communication, residents create and recreate their environments. Ley's participant observation in one inner city area allowed him to identify the nature of those environments, created in situations of considerable uncertainty. (The analogy he uses to describe them is the frontier outpost.) Thus, for example, some streets were perceived as much less safe than others for pedestrians, and were avoided in people's movement patterns, and the area was marked out by graffiti which defined the territories (turfs) of various street gangs (Cybriwsky and Ley, 1974).

Time geography One aspect of the study of the everyday world which became relatively popular in the 1970s was time geography. It was initiated in a paper by Hagerstrand (1970), who argued that in regional science and planning:

> time has to be taken into account along with space . . . time has a critical importance when it comes to fitting people and things together for functioning in socio-economic systems (p. 10).

The constraints on individual behaviour, he argued, are time-space prisms: the maximum areal extents that can be covered in a given time. Such constraints are threefold: capability, relating to man's biological nature (particularly the needs to sleep and to eat) and the tools at his disposal; coupling, which relate to the conjointness of many activities; and authority, those powers exercised over man to keep him in certain places/times and out of others.

Hagerstrand's case was that study of individual biographies would indicate the constraints acting on people, and lead to the potential for better spatial planning. (The affinities with Seamon's work are strong.) It has generated much empirical work on biographies (e.g. Martensson, 1979), which implicitly uses the ideal-typical approach of Schutz and Weber although being much more empirically based. According to Pred (1977, p. 210), Hagerstrand conceived time geography:

> from a humanistic concern with the 'quality of life' and everyday freedom of action implications for individuals of both existing and alternative technologies, institutions, organizations, and urban forms.

and the empirical procedures and findings have been applied in a variety of planning situations in Sweden. Pred suggests that it can also be used in the study of a discipline's intellectual history (see Pred, 1979), in the reinterpretation of historical events, in the study of alienation in society, and in the changing structure of family life. (See also the discussion on p. 103 of structuration.)

Examples of the wider utility of time geography suggested by Pred include a study by Carlstein (1980) which reinterprets the economic geography of pre-industrial societies in terms of time-space resources. However, as developed more in the next chapter, although Carlstein claims that his approach separates essence from appearance (p. 58), the main thrust is structuralist rather than humanist. He makes clear that the approach 'does not . . . subscribe to a phenomenological framework of the 'life-world'. Nor does it entail resting content on an atomistic or behavioural level' (p. 61). Thus time geography has extended much beyond the original formulation, so that in an attempt 'to place time firmly in the minds of human geographers', Parkes and Thrift (1980, p. xi) have adopted a broader perspective which they term chronogeographical. Their treatment is dominantly positivist, indicating a field that is difficult to categorize (as Carlstein, 1980, makes clear); it contains elements, not necessarily integrated in any one piece of work, of all of the approaches discussed in this book.

An evaluation

Humanistic geography is not readily evaluated because, unlike positivist work, it has no explicit criteria by which it can be assessed. The aim is not to increase explanation and predictive power, but to improve understanding, which in a hermeneutical sense is very much a personal project for the observer and, where relevant, the observed. There can be no progress as such, therefore, in that the work is not cumulative. The only real assessment is whether the individuals concerned feel that both their understanding and their future action are better as a result of the work. In an academic discipline this involves a further hermeneutic relationship, between researcher and student, between whom there may be at least one and perhaps several filters (the research paper or monograph; the textbook; the tutor).

Certain humanistic approaches are less atomistic than others, in that they seek to identify 'universal knowledge' or elements of pure consciousness. If such goals were achieved, this would certainly represent an ability to generalize, although it is not clear how such ability would be realized or how the results would be communicated. In any case, as made clear here, with very few exceptions geographers have not attempted to proceed towards 'universal knowledge', and where they have, it has often been in a positivist as much as a humanist perspective (see Gregory, 1978a). This does not obscure the impact of essays and analyses in the humanist tradition. As Entrikin (1976) and others have indicated, these have provided a strong critique to the positivist approaches and have indicated the centrality of intentions and meanings in any study of *human* geography.

The problems of doing research in humanist geography are several, as are those of transmitting its aims and results. One of these, to many by far the most important, is that of communication, in particular the constraints of language. As Olsson has made clear in a number of essays, the human world is full of ambiguity and complexity but language translates much of this into certainty (Olsson, 1978). To him, the humanist approach:

> allows us to grasp both the certainty of the external and the ambiguity of the internal, of jibberish and silent communication. To speak in aid of ambiguity is therefore not to condone obfuscation but rather to be so precise that the inherent contradictions are retained intact (p. 118).

He seeks to avoid dematerializing 'objects into ideas' (Olsson, 1979, p. 304), to develop a social science in which the constraints of language (which is not the only text) do not distort the message. At present he claims, 'what is judged to be true and just is not independent of the language in which that judgement is phrased' (Olsson, 1975, p. 26), a statement which refers not only to written language but also to the majority of analytical tools. Thus the ambiguities of reality should not be distorted by the languages of mathematics and statistics, for example, not only because this hampers the development of understanding but also because it is used (or may be used) as the basis for social engineering (planning) which will confine the world within present boundaries rather than allowing it to change. (See also Pred, 1981a.)

The problem of language, in its broadest sense, is internal to humanistic geography, just as it is to all humanistic enterprises. Other problems refer to the relevance of humanistic approaches and their orientation. The major criticisms are twofold. The first, largely positivist, presents humanistic approaches as subjective and thus unscientific, of general interest perhaps but having little relevance to the creation of better objective conditions in a late capitalist world. The second, largely structuralist, presents the atomistic focus on the individual in humanistic work as a distortion of reality; it gives the individual freedom to act when in fact he or she is very much constrained, if not constricted, by external circumstances over which he or she has little control. A partial response to such criticisms is to claim that some humanistic approaches at least have scientific goals, in that they are seeking to uncover the nature of universal knowledge which governs all individual behaviour. Such goals do not loom large in humanistic geography, however, most of which focuses on the particular and emphasizes the unique. It illustrates the subjectivity and complexity of man and drives home the importance of meanings, but remains a relatively diffuse literature, a critique whose alternative has attracted little support.

The epistemology of humanistic approaches, then, emphasizes the subjectivity of knowledge. Man is a thinking being whose intentionality creates a world within which he or she acts. The ontology of such approaches, therefore, is that knowledge can only be obtained from what exists in the human mind. This involves a variety of levels: the often unconsidered and accepted elements of the taken-for-granted everyday world; the new elements which are brought into the life-world, or behavioural environment; the theories which link these elements together and provide the frameworks for conduct and action; and the components of pure consciousness which structure those theories and the perceptual processes involved in the creation of behavioural environments. Humanistic approaches seek to explore these various levels, to gain an understanding of man. Humanistic geography explores those aspects relative to its major themes: man/environment relationships and man/man interrelationships in their spatial contexts. The understanding achieved is to be used to help individuals understand themselves, thereby increasing the depth of their self-knowledge and enabling them to improve the quality of their lives.

4
Structuralist approaches

The characteristic feature of structuralist approaches is an axiom that explanations for observed phenomena must be sought in general structures which underpin all phenomena but are not identifiable within them; the explanation cannot be produced through empirical study of the phenomena alone. Such beliefs have a very long history. In many religions, for example, the belief that life was created by a god means that the understanding of life requires an understanding of the god's intentions. Recent structuralism argues that the underlying structures can be appreciated through a combination of theory and observation/analysis. The relative importance of the two enterprises varies between different types of structuralism and different structuralists.

The term structuralism is very widely used, throughout the social sciences and humanities. Rossi (1981), for example, distinguishes between empirical and transformational structuralism. The former is characteristic of work, especially in sociology, on social structures, which emphasises interdependence in systems: this is frequently known as structural-functionalism (see p. 45). Transformational structuralism, on the other hand, represents the approaches presented here:

> Transformational structuralists find not only naïve but false the positivist and behaviourist assumptions that people's conscious explanations and overt behavior are to be taken at their face value as objects of scientific analysis . . . we have to go beyond surface structures to find the deep and real structures that account for the variety of observable phenomena or conscious explanations and their apparent contradictions (Rossi, 1981, p. 63).

Thus structuralists believe not only in the need to delve beneath surface appearances to discover explanations but also that such analysis will identify universal structures that provide the motive forces in societies.

Even within the field of transformational structuralism there is a considerable variety of approaches. Not all of these are relevant to the present book. Two types are identified here.

Structure as construct

The basic feature of work in this type is a belief that cultural phenomena – language, kinship rules, myths, taboos, etc – which appear extraordinarily diverse when observed are in fact transformations of a few basic structures which are universal to the human mind. Discovery of those structures involves identifying the nature of human existence itself:

> Cultural and social phenomena . . . are to be thought of as projections onto the world out-there of structured patterns generated by human minds. It is further postulated that, at the most basic, abstract level, the variety of such patterns is very limited. The diverse structured patterns discernible in directly observable cultural phenomena are all transformations of a narrow range of mentalist structures which are common to all humanity (Leach, 1981, p. 29).

Those structures (often called deep structures) are not accessible to social scientific analysis. They must be uncovered through study of their transformations in observable phenomena and behaviour.

The origins of this form of structuralist inquiry are generally traced to the work of de Saussure (1966) in linguistics. In this, he stressed the difference between the signifier – the term used in a particular language – and the signified – the concept which the term represents. He argued that:

> The relationship between signifier and signified is not natural or fixed but social and, hence, infinitely variable. Therefore, the nature of the sign itself is completely arbitrary. Since signifier and signified can take any form and since signs can be combined into an infinite variety of languages, the proper focus on the study of language is on the relational and structural characteristics (Heydebrand, 1981, p. 82).

A further difference emphasized in this linguistic work, and clearly building on the signifier/signified relationship, is that between *parole* (the speech act of everyday life) and *langue* (the language system whose rules are understood so that the speech acts are interpretable). The former is a transformation of the latter: structural linguistics analyses speech, in order to identify the fundamental characteristics of language systems, the rules which govern communication and which are thought to be genetically imprinted.

The development of transformational structuralism in linguistics is associated with the works of Noam Chomsky. He argues that the common principles of languages are so well articulated, and that children can so readily derive the structural principles of their native languages from listening to their parents, that language systems must be 'biologically determined' and 'genetically transmitted from parents to their children' (Lyons, 1977, p. 7). Thus the study of language should be able to transform one into another, thereby isolating the general principles. These principles, which are genetically imprinted, are the deep structures whose identification is the purpose of structuralist inquiry (Smith and Wilson, 1979).

Within the social sciences, the introduction of transformational structuralism is associated in particular with the work of the French social anthropologist Claude Lévi-Strauss. His enterprise was strongly influenced by Saussurean linguistics, and led him to the conclusion that 'human behavior is preordained by unconscious forces beyond human control' (Kurzweil, 1980, p. 27). Identifying those unconscious forces involves studying each example of a particular phenomenon (e.g. myth) as a transformation of a deep structure. Each is an algebraic transformation of all others, analysis should show, so that each is also an algebraic transformation of the deep structure, the biologically imprinted element of the human brain which is manipulated by cultural agency. Thus one has a superstructure, which is the observed realization, the deep structure, which is the construct, and between them the mediating force, which transforms the latter into the former. As Gregory (1978a) demonstrates, Lévi-Strauss presented the transformation process with the analogue of a camshaft driving the cutting machine producing jigsaw puzzles. Each individual jigsaw may have its own particular pattern, so that the transformation has concealed to the student of jigsaws the common element: the deep structure which gears the cams and produces each individual puzzle. As a structuralist, Lévi-Strauss was intent on identifying and understanding the nature of the gearbox.

Lévi-Strauss's views are somewhat similar to those of transcendental phenomenologists and their beliefs in 'pure consciousness' (see p. 57). As Leach (1974, p. 26) presents them:

> since all cultures are the product of human brains, there must be, somewhere beneath the surface, features that are common to all.

This argument can be extended to the study of history which 'offers us images of past societies which were structural transformations of those we know' (p. 15). Further, according to some interpretations, because the transformations are represented by mechanical means (as against statistical, probabilistic, ones in positivist science) once the deep structures are identified prediction should be possible:

> By isolating the deep structures of social systems, mechanical models permit us to relate various systems to each other through transformational operations as well as to predict what changes are produced in the system when one or more of its elements are modified (Rossi, 1981, p. 75).

Thus transformational structuralism is scientific.

Lévi-Strauss's methodology developed that employed in Saussurean linguistics, emphasizing the dynamic as well as synchronic relationships between signifier and signified. The resolution of binary oppositions within myths, for example, allows him to identify their basic elements, which can be projected onto those in other phenomena. The transformations necessary to achieve successful projections lead to the identifications of deep structure. The complex nature of this methodology, and certain aspects of Lévi-Strauss's treatment of evidence, have come under considerable criticism (see Leach, 1974, 1981). This suggests that a sizeable gap has still to be bridged between the theory and practice of transformational structuralism in social anthropology: the idea of deep structure has yet to be transformed, according to many, into a convincing scientific concept.

The influence of Lévi-Strauss on social science has been considerable, especially in France (Kurzweil, 1980). But there, it is argued, the ideas no longer have strong support:

> Some readers might consider the discovery of unconscious texts as superfluous or might be bored by the many intricate analyses. Others may deprecate all the structuralisms because they have not answered the questions of human origins and of existence as they originally promised. Perhaps the aims of the structuralists were unattainable: but they did introduce some intriguing and suggestive modes of analysis (Kurzweil, 1980, pp. 244–245).

One other researcher whose work clearly falls into the 'structure as construct' type is the Swiss philosopher/psychologist Jean Piaget. He defines a structure as a system of transformations, incorporating three key ideas: wholeness, transformation, and self-regulation. It is the characteristic of wholeness that distinguishes a structure from an aggregate; in the former every member is linked to every other but in the latter, because of its arbitrariness, this is not so. The idea of transformation is similar to that presented by Chomsky and Lévi-Strauss:

> If the character of structured wholes depends on their laws of composition, these laws must of their very nature be *structuring*: it is the constant duality, or bipolarity, of always being simultaneously *structuring* and *structured* that accounts for the success of the notion of law or rule employed by structuralists (Piaget, 1971, p. 10).

Finally, self-regulation implies that the transformations refer only to the structure itself. It is a closed system in which the transformations act to maintain equilibrium.

In his discussion of structuralism and structures, Piaget (1971, Chapter 6) distinguishes clearly between two types. Global structuralism relates to the study of self-regulating wholes, such as social groups: such structures are simply unions of components (and their study is the structural-functionalism referred to on p. 45). Analytical structuralism, on the other hand, refers to wholes whose constitution is derived from some particular source, a deep structure. Global structuralism, then, refers to theoretical constructs imposed on some subject matter, whereas analytical structuralism refers to wholes which are empirically given – they exist.

Piaget's own work is on analytical structuralism and involves the search for structures which govern the development of intelligence in humans. He views man as starting with a structure, a mode of intellectual functioning, which comprises the ability to do two things: to assimilate new material into existing schema, and to accommodate schemas to experience of the external world (see Boden, 1979). With these twin abilities learning proceeds as a continuing process of transformation. The result is greater intelligence and an ability to act within the empirical world. Thus:

> Whereas other animals cannot alter themselves except by changing their species, man can transform himself by transforming the world and can structure himself by constructing structures; and these structures are his own, for they are not externally predestined either from within or without (Piaget, 1971, pp. 118–119).

Thus Piaget, unlike some phenomenologists, does not believe that there are certain innate essences to human consciousness. Instead, what is innate is the ability to assimilate and to accommodate. With this ability, which forms the initial structure, learning and behaviour take place and the structure is continuously transformed as a consequence. Piaget has demonstrated how such transformations occur as intelligence is acquired, in particular how children learn.

Structure as process

Whereas transformational structuralists included in the 'structure as construct' type present observed phenomena (signifiers) as representations of deep structures genetically imprinted on human consciousness, those discussed here present phenomena as representations of underlying social structures whose base lies in the material conditions of existence. No attempt is made to link these structures to deep structures. The general argument is the same, therefore, except that: first, the transformations are of a structure that is identified at the societal (the infrastructure or base) rather than the neural level; and second, the structure is itself continually being transformed, hence the designation of the type 'structure as process'. These lead to many other differences in approach to understanding and in the nature of analysis.

By far the largest body of literature characterized by the 'structure as process' typification is that of Marxism; this has had most influence on contemporary geography. As a major chronicler of Marxist literature has pointed out 'There is scarcely any question relating to the interpretation of Marxism that is not a matter of dispute' (Kolakowski, 1978, v. 1., p. vi). All that can be done here is to outline the basic features of the Marxist approach to understanding society, plus those of allied developments which are relevant to contemporary work in human geography.

Marxism, historical materialism, and social science
The voluminous writings of Karl Marx — many of them comprising incomplete manuscripts published by others long after his death — have been the stimulus for a great deal of thought and practice. A variety of stimuli have been derived, and Giddens (1979, p. 150ff) has recognized seven different interpretations of Marx's works (in passing, it might be noted that some Marxist scholars, led by Louis Althusser, have identified a clear break in the nature of Marx's work around 1857: Kurzwell, 1980, p. 42): as a methodological prescription for historical analysis; as a means of studying human life; as an emphasis on the significance of labour in human society; as a theory of social change; as a theory of the relationships between superstructure and infrastructure; as a theory of human consciousness; and as a theory of the centrality of class-divisions and class conflict in capitalist society. These to some extent overlap, and are for from mutually exclusive.

The origins of Marx's works lie in his philosophical training and in his own form of humanism. Man, according to his observations and analyses, was becoming dehumanized. Marx's goal was to restore man's humanity to him, by uncovering the workings of dehumanizing society and depicting them in such a way that man would react and create a new, more human world. Thus his work was:

> aimed at enlightening the proletariat concerning its objective and potentially emancipatory role in history (Sensat, 1979, p. 69)

and:

> Marx's criticism of existing society makes sense only in the context of his vision of a new world in which the social significance of each individual's life is directly evident to him (Kolakowski, 1978, v. 1., p. 131).

Central to Marx's analysis of dehumanization in society was the concept of *alienation*. By this he meant the separation of the worker from his own labour power and from its fruits. Labour, under capitalism, is a commodity to be bought and sold, on the market place, and as such is alienated from the worker. Alienation is increased as the division of labour becomes finer. Such dehumanization affects both parties in a capitalist society (i.e. bourgeoisie and proletariat):

> In capitalist production neither the worker nor the capitalist is a human being: their personal qualities have been taken away from them. Thus, when the class-consciousness of the proletariat evolves . . . to a revolutionary consciousness . . . by the same token a worker becomes a human individual once again . . . As for the capitalists, they cannot as a class take up arms against their own dehumanization, since they rejoice in it and in the wealth and power it brings.

Thus, although both sides are equally dehumanized, only the wageearner is spurred by this state of affairs to protestation and social combat (Kolakowski, 1978, v. 1., p. 287).

It is, therefore, the nature of capitalist society that creates alienation according to Marx. Alienation affects all members of the society, but only the proletariat suffer economic as well as human deprivation, however, so only the proletariat can be stimulated to overthrow the capitalist system and create a newer, more human society.

The form of economic analysis developed by Marx was based on earlier work by David Ricardo on the labour theory of value (for a brief introduction to Marxian economics, see Smith, 1981). In a capitalist economic system, the individual must sell his or her labour power in order to obtain a level of subsistence, thereby to reproduce that labour power and to reproduce society as a whole. Labour is sold to a capitalist, who uses it to produce saleable goods. The aim of the capitalist is to sell the goods for as high a price as possible, while keeping the costs of labour as low as possible. The difference between the two, generally known as the *surplus value*, is the return to the capitalist, and is the source of profit. Thus surplus value is the difference between the selling price of a commodity and the production costs, a combination of the costs of labour and those of 'dead labour' (the costs of machinery, materials, etc.) produced by labour earlier in the production chain. The rate of profit is the surplus value divided by total costs (labour plus dead labour).

The aim of capitalists, according to Marx, is to maximize the rate of profit: 'the insatiable appetite for self-increased by the exploitation of surplus labour' (Kolakowski, 1978, v. 1., p. 291). Part of the surplus value accruing to the capitalist class is used for consumption and is spent on the products of the labour process. The remainder is invested in further production, creating further surplus and allowing extended reproduction of the capitalist class. Capitalists seek unendingly to increase their store of wealth, to accumulate.

To achieve their ends, capitalists must hold the costs of labour as low as possible, relative to selling prices. To do this, for any particular commodity, they seek to reduce the unit costs of labour by increasing its productivity (the amount of surplus value produced per unit of labour cost). This is achieved by increased investment in dead labour, in particular in machinery which is more productive than is human labour *per se*. Technological development is therefore vital to the continued expansion of capital. To increase the level of surplus value and the rate of profit the capitalist must always be investing in means of revolutionizing the means of production.

This apparently never-ending process of technological development is far from smooth, however, and the progress of capitalism is punctuated by a series of crises. This is because, as outlined further below, capitalism is characterized by a number of internal contradictions. For example, it seeks to increase the productivity of labour, which means reducing the labour input to the production of each item. At the same time, it seeks to increase the volume of surplus value, which can only be done by increasing the labour force, since labour is the sole source of value (Shaw, 1978, pp. 86–87). The two are only possible if the market for products is increasing, at a rate at least equal to the increase in the volume of production made possible by technological developments. And the market, at least in part, comprises those workers whose wages are being held down by the technological developments that are making many of them under- if not unemployed.

A consequence of these contradictions is the tendency within capitalist economic systems for the rate of profit to decline. This can happen in individual industries and sectors of an economy, as the increased abilities to produce exceed the ability to sell. This leads the capitalists in that sector to withdraw investment from perceived poor potential returns, and to redirect their money into other sectors, where the potential for profitability is perceived to be greater. At the same time, within any sector the more successful capitalists will be able to increase their market share by elimination of competitors. In general, therefore, as the rate of profit in an industry/sector declines so ownership there is concentrated into fewer hands and the surplus realized is redirected into other industries/sectors.

A capitalist system is characterized by flows of capital (the accumulations of surplus value not used by the capitalist class in consumption) from industry to industry in search of high profit rates. The capitalist class, according to Marx, is not concerned with what it produces, and its utility, but only with the profit that it achieves. But this flow of capital produces a tendency for the profit rates in the various industries/sectors to converge on an average. This can lead to crises that are more general than those already mentioned: they affect most, if not all, sectors of an economy and produce a general problem of over-production. The capitalist system has developed the ability to produce commodities far in excess of its ability to consume them (with the latter in part reflecting the increased concentration and centralization of capital and the relatively small proportion of the exchange value of commodities returned to the proletariat to spend on consumption). It must, then, seek to restructure itself, to recreate conditions where profits can be made and investment is worthwhile. To some extent, as already stressed, such restructuring is continuous. But not entirely so. There are occasional major crises, according to Marx's interpretation:

> Capital overcomes its contradictions by means of periodic crises of overproduction which ruin the mass of small owners and wreak havoc among the working

class, after which the balance of the market is restored for a time (Kolakowski, 1978, v. 1., p. 299).

The havoc wreaked on the working class created what Marx termed its immiseration. He believed that capitalism degrades the worker, even though his material conditions of existence may be improved. He becomes increasingly a commodity to be traded, a minute element in the complex division of labour. Alienation is the result of the commodity fetishism that characterizes capitalism: everything is reduced to monetary terms and human dignity is lost. Such alienation can only be removed by the introduction of communism.

In analysing how this dehumanizing alienation is necessary to capitalist expansion, Marx focused on the *dialectics* of the mode of production, on the resolution of contradictory opposites that is central to capitalism's success. (It is the centrality of these contradictions to Marxian economics which' leads to its typification here as structure as process: the structure contains ongoing processes.) Thus Marx's approach to analysis, usually known as *historical materialism*, is based on understanding the dialectics at work within the structure.

The concept of dialectics was developed by Marx from his work with Hegel's phenomenology. It is usually presented as a sequence of thesis, antithesis, synthesis, with the sequence being replicated as each synthesis in turn becomes a thesis. The thesis is something of only limited value which generates opposition to itself: the antithesis. The struggle between the two eventually leads to an accommodation, a synthesis that incorporates the best elements of the two but which, in turn, generates its own opposition. (For an introduction to dialectics in philosophy, see Popper, 1972, pp. 312ff.) Such oppositions, or contradictions, appeared to Marx to characterize capitalism (as exemplified above). Their resolution, through the creation of new syntheses, provided the generative force for continued capitalist accumulation. (In Marxist dialectics, the term contradictions is not used in the same way as it is in everyday speech. Heilbroner (1980) notes, for example, that dialectical contradictions are not the same as logical contradictions (i.e. assertions each of which denies the other). Rather they imply incompatibility; as Heilbroner (p. 35) puts it, 'the unstable coexistence and successive resolution of incompatible forces'. Things begin as the resolution of incompatible forces, but they immediately set up a new pair of such forces.)

In Marx's work, the major dialectic identified was that between the productive forces and the relations of production (Shaw, 1978, p. 8). It is realized in the falling rate of profit:

> the urge to maximise the rate of profit defeats its own object by increasing the amount of constant capital [dead labour] and so causing the profit rate to fall steadily (Kolakowski, 1978, v. 1., p. 322)

which in turn creates inter-class (proleteriat-bourgeoisie) antagonism. In Hegelian dialectics, every synthesis took one closer to pure consciousness (in the phenomenological sense of that term: see p. 57). In Marxian dialectics, the uncovering of every successive synthesis should reveal its real conditions to the proletarian consciousness (as against the false consciousness that capitalism itself creates), and lead to the revolutionary explosion that will finally remove capitalism.

The concepts of productive forces and relations of production are central to historical materialism and its analysis of capitalist development. The *productive forces* are the elements of the production process. They combine the means of production, the objective conditions of labour, and labour power (within which is incorporated scientific and other knowledge). The *relations of production* comprise the conditions within which the productive forces are brought into operation. These create the work situation and are based on ownership relationships; the capitalist owns the means of production and buys the labour power of the proletariat in order to create commodities and surplus value. These relations (for a full exposition see Shaw, 1978) are fundamentally class relations: each society has a privileged class with regard to ownership of the productive forces, and an underprivileged, exploited proletariat.

The dialectic between these two elements involves the resolution of the contradictions which capitalism necessarily creates, as the desire to create surplus value founders on the falling rate of profit, the replacement of labour (the source of surplus value) by dead labour, and the limits to markets. To overcome these limits to the accumulation of wealth, the capitalist class uses the relations of production to reorganize its use of the productive forces, seeking ways out of crises by creating new forms of profitability. This setting of the productive forces in motion involves exploitation of the proletariat by the bourgeoisie, and the antagonism which this generates is itself a continuing problem in the realization of surplus value. Resolution of this antagonism, or at least its containment, involves the creation of a social formation, a societal structure (usually including a state) in which there is sufficient harmony that the relations of production are able to employ the forces. (Such a structure legitimizes capitalist relations.)

Historical materialism, as developed by Marx, thus involves a dialectical process. The social formation comprises a series of oppositions or contradictory forces, which frequently hinder the achievement of its goals. Such contradictions must be circumvented, by the creation of new situation that will encourage and allow further pursuit of the goals. The restrictions on the use of the productive forces are in some way removed, so as to allow surplus value to be appropriated. But, because the capitalist system permanently comprises contradictory tendencies, this new synthesis is of necessity short-lived. It soon generates its own opposites, and creates further crises of over-production and over-accumulation. Thus capitalism is continually transforming itself. (Note that historical materialism as an academic discipline cannot predict the way in which any individual contradiction is resolved. Thus the processes of change cannot be subject to a positivist analysis, since they cannot be expressed as a functioning system, p. 41: the forces of change are not exdogenously determined.)

Marx's work on dialectics was continued by his collaborator, Engels, from whose work three 'laws of the dialectic' have been derived (Kolakowski, 1978, v. 1., p. 388ff). The first is that *quantity becomes quality*. Quantitative differences, when they reach a certain threshold, become qualitative ones, as when a sum of money is large enough to be invested to produce surplus value, and thereby becomes capital. Secondly, *development proceeds by contradiction and the interpenetration of opposites*. Nature is a system of tensions and conflicts whose resolution define the next stage of nature. Finally, there is the law of *the negation of the negation*:

> every system has a natural tendency to produce out of itself another system which is its contrary; this 'negation' is negated in its turn so as to produce a system that is in some important respects a repitition of the first, but on a higher level (Kolakowski, 1978, v. 1, p. 392).

Thus society, like a plant, reproduces itself in a more perfect form, in that it has overcome the current negation: development is a spiralling process. These three laws refine the presentation of historical materialism. The seeds of change within a society are contained in the contradictory tendencies within it, so that the process of development is the result of the resolution of contradictions.

The whole of Marx's work was organized to indicate the crucial role of the economic structure of capitalist society – in particular the various contradictions involving the productive forces and the relations of production – as determinants of human consciousness and being. To some, this led to an interpretation that denied human free will and relegated culture and politics to the status of dependent categories. Marxist structuralism separates the infrastructure (the economic determinants) from the superstructure (the religion, culture, polity etc.) of a society. It does not entirely relegate the latter to a position of total dependence on the former:

> Marxist structuralists insist that the different structures which constitute any given social formation all have a certain autonomy, and that while the economic structure (the mode of production) has to be conceived as ultimately determinant, other structures may nevertheless be *dominant* in constituting and reproducing a particular form of society (Bottomore, 1978, p. 137).

Thus, the nature of the state in a particular place at a particular time may influence how a current economic crisis is solved. But the state does not determine the nature of society, it only influences the realization of the processes that are embedded in the economic infrastructure.

Historical materialism is not, therefore, a crude form of economic determinism. Marx argued that economic forces dominate capitalist society, but not that there is no freedom for human interpretation of those forces in the resolution of particular antagonisms. Thus the much quoted statement from *The Eighteenth Brumaire of Louis Bonaparte* that:

> Men make their own history, but they do not make it just as they please; they do not make it in circumstances chosen by themselves, but under circumstances directly found, given and transmitted from the past.

The unfolding of history is the result of the conscious behaviour of individuals. Marx's case is that the nature of that consciousness is determined by the economic circumstances, which in turn, as the result of successive dialectic syntheses, are determined by earlier economic circumstances. Thus:

> great individuals who appear to shape the course of history actually come upon the scene because society needs them. Alexander, Cromwell and Napoleon are instruments of the historical process; they may affect it by their accidental personal traits, but they are unconscious agents of a great impersonal force which they did not create. The effectiveness of their action is determined by the situation in which it takes place (Kolakowski, 1978, v. 1, p. 340).

Marx's aim, then, was to uncover the general laws of history – its immanent forces, which he located in the economic infrastructure – and not to account for specific events. As Kolakowski (p. 339) puts it, historical materialism:

> is not and does not claim to be a key to the interpretation of any particular historical event. All it does is define the relations between some, but by no means all, features of social life.

One of those essential features is the class division of society, so that the whole unfolding of history, including the development of the superstructure of individual social formations, reflects the antagonisms of that division. This is often interpreted as history being created by the class struggle. To some, the validity of this general concept of history means that 'Marx's approach is still the only one which enables us to explain the whole span of human history' (Hobsbawm, 1972, p. 282).

Because historical materialism as conceived by Marx is not concerned with the details of history, it is not an empirical science. As such, it differs from the structure as construct type discussed earlier, within which the nature of the structure can be identified by analysis of its transformations in particular empirical situations:

> For Marx, the scientific understanding of the capitalist system consists in the discovery of the internal structure hidden behind its visible functioning (Godelier, 1972, pp. 335–336).

This hidden structure, Godelier argues, cannot be apprehended in its realization, because capitalism is not a thing but a social relationship. As a result, the structures which are sought by historical materialists are relationships (hence the definition 'structure as process'). What is observed by empirical social science research is an outcome of those processes, which cannot themselves be apprehended.

Because historical materialism is concerned with hidden structures, its 'explanations' are not subject to empirical verification. Its method is the development of conjectural theory (Saunders, 1981, p. 17). This proposes certain relationships within society which, if correct, would account for empirical appearances. The theory is consistent with observation. This is termed the retroductive method (Sayer, 1979), which is neither deductive (there are no laws which are ahistorical, only historical processes) nor inductive (regularities in the world of appearances provide no basis for implying regularities in the causes). Thus Marx's historical materialism involves the development and refinement of plausible theories about the dominant forces in society, plausible both as explanations and as guides to action:

> Marx's method can be used fruitfully to generate theories that are plausible to a greater or lesser extent but can never finally be demonstrated, and it follows that there is no necessary and compelling reason to accept such theories other than one's own political values and purposes. Marxism, in other words, is as much a guide to political practice as a method of scientific analysis (Saunders, 1981, p. 18).

Other theories may be equally plausible.

Developments on Marxism

The published works of Marx (and of his collaborator, Engels) have been more influential than those of most other scholars, over a very wide field. The impacts can be divided into two types. The first involves Marxism as a guide to political practice, with regard to both the revolutionary potential of the proletariat and the criteria for a society in which human dignity is not degraded. A large number of revolutionaries and would-be revolutionaries have based their programmes on Marx (see, for example, the review in Kolakowski, 1978, v. 2), although, as Kolakowski (1978, v. 3) shows, attempts to apply Marxist ideas have largely abused them, in part, he claims, because they have been allied with nationalist ideology:

> Wherever Communism is in power, the ruling class transforms it into an ideology whose real sources are nationalism, racism, or imperialism ... Nationalism lives only as an ideology of hate, envy, and thirst for power (Kolakowski, 1978, v. 3, pp. 529–530).

Because of this, he claims, Marxism as practice has lost contact with the other main stream of Marxist literature identified here: Marxism as a theoretical base for the social sciences. The latter is in general a relatively recent development, with the volume of Marxist scholarship expanding very substantially since the Second World War, especially in the English-speaking world.

To many Marxists, the distinction made here between Marxist practice and Marxist social science is unreal. Adoption of a Marxist approach implies that scholars are working not simply to provide a proper understanding of the course of human history, but also to achieve a transformation from capitalism to socialism. To others, however, whereas the former task is quite acceptable the other is not (for a variety of reasons). These may be termed Marxian writers, in that they use the basic methods of Marxist analysis. The lack of commitment to Marx's political programme is sometimes explicit, but often only implicit. His concept of historical materialism, and especially the centrality of the class conflict contradiction, is used to indicate the poverty of competing paradigms. Thus:

> Orthodox economics tries to show that markets allocate scarce resources according to relative efficiency; political economics tries to show that markets distribute income according to relative power (Nell, 1972, p. 95).

Work in the Marxian mould has considerably extended the original analyses, which is not surprising, if the theory of historical materialism is correct, since the continued dialectic of the structure as process has created many new social forms that were unforeseen by Marx. To some, the fact that these were unforeseen is indicative of the failure of Marxism as a theory. Popper (1972, p. 37), for example, claims that many of its predictions have been tested and refuted, but:

> instead of accepting the refutations the followers of Marx re-interpreted both the theory and the evidence in order to make them agree. In this way they rescued the theory from refutation; but they did so at the price of adopting a device which made it irrefutable.

To him, Marxism failed to meet the criteria for designation as a science. (See also Popper, 1945.) To others, Marx never made any prediction of a socialist revolution, beyond claiming that it would be generated by 'the catastrophe towards which capitalism is swiftly yet unconsciously tending' (Kolakowski, 1978, v. 1, p. 306). According to Marx's thesis:

> Only the proletariat can intervene to redress the conflict between the productive forces and their relations of production . . . In the absence of this, the productive forces will continue to push for more compatible relations of production (Shaw, 1978, p. 113).

The analysis of these pushes for 'more compatible relations of production' has been the focus of much recent Marxist social science, concerned with such topics as the rise of the state, the changing structure of ownership, the evolution of late capitalism, and the growth of 'intermediate classes', all of which were only dimly perceived by Marx in the mid-nineteenth century.

While some practising Marxists seek to create the socialist revolution, therefore, and some academic Marxists seek to generate the conditions for it by their analyses and teaching, the main impact of Marx's work on academic social science in the capitalist world has been via the introduction of Marxian perspectives, in some cases modified to incorporate aspects of others. (That individual social scientists, as social scientists, appear to be Marxian rather than Marxist, as defined here, does not involve comment on their political philosophy. It simply indicates that their social science work concentrates on historical materialist analysis and makes little or no reference to any political programme.) Of these perspectives, three are outlined here because of their usage in and relevance to the literature in human geography.

Realism More properly, transcendental realism, to distinguish it from naïve or direct realism – p. 26) is a philosophical position associated with the works of Bhaskar (1975, 1979) and Keat and Urry (1975). Set in a clear structuralist mould:

> The basic principle of realist philosophy of science, viz. that perceptions gives us access to things and experimental activity access to structures that exist independently of us, is very simple (Bhaskar, 1975, p. 9).

Underlying this basic principle is a belief that mechanisms are independent of the events that they generate. Constant conjunctions of events may provide the bases for empirical laws, but not for process or mechanism laws (those which create the conditions for the operation of the empirical laws). Such process laws are:

> the real things and structures, mechanisms and processes, events and possibilities of the world; and for the most part they are quite independent of us . . . They are the intransitive, science-independent, objects of scientific observation and discovery (Bhaskar, 1975, p. 22).

Thus, according to this view, in much scientific activity the relationships identified reflect the nature of the experiments conducted, which are at the level of appearances and not that of the mechanisms which produce those experiences. (Gravity exists independently of experiments that show its relationship to the rate of acceleration of falling bodies, for example. The results of those experiments are neither necessary nor sufficient for an understanding of the causal laws producing gravity; they are illustrations of it.) Thus transcendental realism involves the study of a 'law-governed world independent of man' (p. 26):

> Science, then, is the systematic attempt to express in thought the structures and ways of acting of things that exist and act independently of thought. The world is structured and complex and not made for men. It is entirely accidental that we exist, and understand something about our bit of it (p. 250).

In *A Realist Theory of Science* Bhaskar (1975) argues that the purpose of science is to isolate the general laws of nature that operate independently of man's existence and his creations (including scientific experiments). In this sense they are laws of the structure and not of the relationships in the superstructure (see Keat and Urry, 1975, pp. 30–31 who argue that the answers to 'why' questions are to be found in 'how' and 'what' questions: 'to explain why is partly to say how' – p. 31). In *The Possibility of Naturalism* Bhaskar (1979) applies these ideas to what he terms 'the contemporary human sciences'. In that context, the realist philosophy involves:

> the movement from the manifest phenomena of social life, as conceptualized in the experience of the social agents concerned, to the essential relations that necessitate them (p. 32).

Thus the focus is not on people and what they do (and why they say they do it) but rather on the structures of the societies of which they are part and which provide the necessary conditions for their activity: structure is separated from action. (The former, according to Bhaskar, are the psychological sciences; the latter are the social sciences.)

In developing his realist approach to the social sciences, Bhaskar is clearly influenced by the content of Marxist analysis ('if Marxism without detailed social scientific and historical work is empty, then such work without Marxism (or some such theory) is blind' – p. 56) and its retroductive methodology (see p. 99). He argues against both idealism – separation of the superstructure from the infrastructure, or effects from their causes, and reductionism – which represents the superstructure as a mechanical outcome of processes in the infrastructure. If the infrastructure is the social formation (complete with its antagonisms, as identified by Marx) and the superstructure contains its individuals, then not only does the society guide the actions of individuals, through the processes of socialization, but in addition the actions of the individuals are part of the process of the reproduction and transformation of society. In this way, human agency is incorporated into the dialectic, so that there is both a dialectic within the infrastructure (between the productive forces and the relations of production) and between the infrastructure and the superstructure (between the process and its realization). Thus a transcendental realist philosophy of social science seeks the causes of phenomena in a structure which is constantly being transformed but, more so than is the case in many Marxist presentations, argues that the outcomes of these causes in turn influence the processes of transformation within the infrastructure. The individual cannot exist without society (so the superstructure is dependent on the infrastructure) but in addition society can neither exist nor be continually re-created without the activities of individuals.

The basic argument of transcendental realism, therefore, is that the empirical world is the result of the operation of processes that cannot be observed. All that is possible is analysis which can indicate that observation is in line with the theory of those processes (this is the retroductive method – p. 99). In physical science, this involves conducting experiments which demonstrate relationships (notably cause-effect claims) that confirm the theory. Because the laws of the physical world are unaffected by the existence of man and his study of their outcomes, this means that the same experiment, whenever conducted, should produce the same result, if the available theory is valid. (This is not to deny that the universe is invariant over time; the sun is cooling, for example, but change can also be represented in the theory.) In realist terms, therefore, the same conjunction of events (an experimental situation) can be created many times, with the same outcome. In social science, on the other hand, there are no invariant elements within the infrastructure. It is a process itself, so that conjunctions cannot be repeated. Because of this, relationships within the superstructure, the empirical world, are not constant, which means that empirical laws cannot be derived. All that is possible is description of the present conjuncture, which will not be repeated. (It is for this reason that realists are anti-positivist in their philosophy.) Thus whereas realist physical scientists can continue to design experiments to test hypotheses and produce theories in the knowledge that there are universal laws of matter waiting to be uncovered, realist social scientists must work in a situation in which the causes are always changing, in part through their effects which feed back, so that behaviour in the future is in part constrained by behaviour in the past and its representation in the landscape. (This difference between physical and social science leads to the realist rejection of systems analysis in human geography (Gregory, 1980). A system, in structural-functionalist theory, is a particular construction of elements and links within which change follows a particular direction; a structure, in a realist philosophy, is forever changing, so that the elements and links change. A systems view freezes change. A realist view focuses on it.)

Bhaskar's realist philosophy has much in common with the theory of **structuration**, developed by the Cambridge sociologist Anthony Giddens. This theory was developed, he indicates, because of:

> the lack of a theory of action in the social sciences . . . In their eagerness to 'get behind the backs' of the social actors whose conduct they seek to understand . . . [Marxist and related approaches] largely ignore just those phenomena that action philosophy makes central to human conduct (Giddens, 1979, p. 2).

Human action takes place within structural contexts, however, and the relevance of Marxist work to the understanding of these is made clear: 'Marx's writings still represent the most significant single fund of ideas that can be drawn upon in seeking to illuminate problems of agency and structure' (Giddens, 1979, p. 53; see also Giddens, 1981). But the problem with much structuralism – both Marxist or 'structuralism as process' and 'structuralism as construct' – he argues, is that it gives too little attention to the role of human agency:

> The production of society . . . is always and everywhere a skilled accomplishment of its members . . . [but it is necessary] to reconcile such an emphasis with the equally essential thesis . . . that if men make society, they do not do so merely under conditions of their own choosing (Giddens, 1976, p. 126).

The aim of Giddens' work is to fuse structuralist approaches to society, with their focus on the constraints to behaviour, to humanistic approaches, whose foci are the intentional acts of human agency. This fusion is achieved through his concept of structuration:

> the duality of structure, which relates to the fundamentally recursive character of social life, and expresses the mutual dependence of structure and agency . . . the structural properties of social systems are both the medium and the outcome of the practices that constitute those systems (Giddens, 1979, p. 69).

Thus rather than see structure as a constraint to action, Giddens presents it is *simultaneously both constraining and enabling*, whilst at the same time it is being reproduced and transformed by individuals. (Any approach which denies the role of individual actors is teleological according to Giddens and 'implies a derogation of the lay actor[s] . . . [who] are regarded as cultural dopes or mere 'bearers of a mode of production', with no worthwhile understanding of their surroundings or the circumstances of their action', Giddens, 1979, p. 71.)

Giddens' theory of structuration is based on a series of clearly stated 'rules of sociological method', which can be taken as axioms. They are (Giddens, 1976, pp. 160–162):

1 'Sociology is not concerned with a 'pre-given' universe of objects, but with one which is constituted or produced by the active doings of subjects.'
2 'The production and reproduction of society thus has to be treated as a skilled performance on the part of its members not as merely a mechanical series of processes.'
3 'The realm of human agency is bounded. Men produce society, but they do so as historically located actors, and not under conditions of their own choosing.'
4 'Structures must not be conceptualized as simply placing constraints upon human agency, but as enabling.'
5 'Processes of structuration involve an interplay of meanings, norms, and power.'
6 'The sociological observer cannot make social life available as a 'phenomenon' for observation independently of drawing upon his knowledge of it as a resource whereby he constitutes it as a 'topic for investigation'.'

7 'Immersion in a form of life is the only and necessary means whereby an observer is able to generate such characterizations.'
8 'Sociological concepts thus obey what I call a double hermeneutic.' (The first is the nature of scientific activity itself; the second involves using science to interpret a different conception of the universe held by the individuals being studied.)
9 'In sum, the primary tasks of sociological analysis are the following: 1 The hermeneutic explication and mediation of divergent forms of life within descriptive metalanguages of social science; 2 Explication of the production and reproduction of society as the accomplished outcome of human agency.'

For such a merger of the 'structure as process' and humanistic approaches, he identified three concepts regarding society: first, the *system*, or set of regular social practices; second, the *structure*, the (changing) rules and resources which guide the system; and third, *structuration*, the conditions whereby members of systems govern the continuity and/or transformation of structures, and thereby influence the reproduction of the systems themselves. What Giddens is proposing, therefore, is the development of a mode of analysis which pays substantial attention to the role of human agency in the transformation of structures. (Gregory, 1978a, p. 89, claims that the concept of structuration is taken directly from Marx, 1976, p. 283; the statement there, however, refers to a dialectic between man and nature rather than man and structure.) Structuration accepts part at least of the Marxist arguments regarding the role of the infrastructure, but argues for the important role of human agency in both the realization of the structural processes (i.e. the observed world of the empirical researcher) and the modification of the processes themselves.

Critical theory The final 'school of thought' to be discussed here is also associated with Marxism in many ways and has the same basic goals. (Kolakowski – 1978, v. 3, p. 357 – characterizes it as a truncated and partial Marxism.) It is not a single body of work associated with an individual scholar, but rather a large body of linked material produced by a group of scholars frequently known as the 'Frankfurt School'. This is divided into two groups, the first focused on five scholars working at the Institute of Social Research at Frankfurt before the Second World War and the second centred on the work since the 1950s of Jurgen Habermas.

The common aims of the critical theorists are similar to those of Marx: the creation of a society lacking domination. Individuals must be emancipated, therefore, by a process:

> involving the active participation of everyone in the control of social phenomena; in other words, people must be subjects and not objects (Kolakowski, 1978, v. 3, p. 392).

This emancipation from domination, Habermas argues, must be achieved through:

> self-reflection, [whereby] individuals can become aware of forces which have exerted a hitherto unacknowledged influence over them. Thus, the act of knowing coincides with the goal of the interest (Held, 1980, p. 318).

The emancipatory interest, then, is achieved by increasing individual awareness. Successful self-reflection leads to a greater conscious understanding of the nature of one's position in society and therefore to an increased ability to realize emancipation through changing society.

Only self-reflection, according to Habermas, can create the conditions for, the achievement of real, material freedom (conditions which are necessary but not sufficient). The role of critical science is to pave the way for this process. Self-knowledge is hindered, it is claimed, by the various interests of individuals and groups within society. Positivist science, for example, advances certain technical interests based in the desire for domination, whereas the hermeneutic sciences seek to advance intersubjective understanding. With regard to the latter, much communication within a social system is distorted, in part because of 'the semantic structure of communication itself' (Sensat, 1979, p. 27). Critical theory seeks to remove those distortions by the creation of what Habermas calls the *ideal speech situation*. In this, there is:

> equal opportunity for discussion, free from all domination, whether arising from conscious strategic behaviour and/or systematically distorted communication (Held, 1980, pp. 343–344).

Critical theorists have examined a wide range of phenomena to demonstrate the variety of distortions in communication which manipulate knowledge to particular interests. (Studies of aesthetics, for example, illustrate the influence of bourgeois culture.) The aim is to extend Marxism, and to show, as in Habermas' (1976) *Legitimation Crisis*, that the transformations of society since Marx wrote have created new conditions relating to the maintenance of a capitalist structure. This involves studying the role of the state (a topic largely ignored by Marx):

> In order for the system to function, there must be a general compliance with the laws, rules etc. Although this compliance can be secured to a limited extent by coercion, societies claiming to operate according to the principles of bourgeois democracy depend more on the existence of a widespread belief that the system adheres to the principles of equality, justice and freedom. Thus the capitalist state must act to support the production process and at the same time act, if it is to preserve its image as fair and just, to conceal what it is doing. If man's loyalty is threatened, a tendency toward a legitimation crisis is established (Held, 1980, p. 291).

The act of concealment is part of the systematically distorted communication identified by Habermas. Emancipation will enable people to overcome this situation, to provide enlightenment via self-reflection and undistorted discourse. Thus:

> The Frankfurt school and Habermas sought to extend and adapt the insights of Marx's work in order to reveal the complex factors which hinder people coming to consciousness of themselves as capable of different action (Held, 1980, p. 363).

Critical theory, then, is Marxist both in its analysis and in its commitment to practical goals. It seeks to uncover what the processes are within a society (hence it is realist) and to communicate the results to individuals so that they will better realize how they are manipulated in a society and as a result wish to change that situation.

Structuralism in human geography

As with the positivist and humanistic approaches, the introduction of structuralist ideas to human geography came via the other social sciences, most of which were either the source of structuralist developments or had been influenced by them earlier than geography. And, as also with the other two approaches, it is possible to find examples of the importation of some structuralist ideas to human geography long before the main impact in the 1970s (see Johnston, 1983a, chap. 6). Indeed, two early anarchists – Peter Kropotkin (Breitbart, 1981), and Elisee Reclus (Dunbar, 1981) – were both practising geographers.

With regard to the schools of work depicted here as 'structuralism as construct' there has been little attempt to relate most of them to the research interests of human geographers. Gregory (1978a) has presented a brief outline of Lévi-Strauss's work and related it to human geography, but this has not been taken further. Perhaps surprisingly, the structuralist work in social anthropology has not had any impact on cultural geography, as illustrated by the absence of any reference to it in either a review essay by Mikesell (1978) or a programmatic essay on the economic geography of non-industrial societies by Jones (1978).

The only 'structure as construct' work to have had much influence on geographical research is that of Piaget on the acquisition of intelligence as a process of structural transformation. This developmental psychology work included studies of how the child learns about space and geometry. He found that each stage of development is qualitatively different from that preceding it, and that at each stage new material is integrated with that already held, that all material is consolidated and co-ordinated – this is the self-regulating feature of the structure in that all of the material is fitted into schemata (it is not random information). Piaget's experiments suggested that there are four major stages in the development of a child's conception of space (a review is provided by Hart and Moore, 1973). These experiments did not extend to the traditional subject matter of geography. Gould (1973, p. 185) notes that:

> Though much of the pioneering work of the child psychologist Piaget is directly concerned with the way in which children learn about space, the world around them, and geometrical and topological concepts . . ., it does not deal with the essentially *geographic* images that children hold or the way they learn about them.

Gould's own work was very largely concerned with 'preference surfaces' (see Golledge, 1981), the attitudes of respondents to particular places (Gould and White, 1974), but others have been more concerned with the child's acquisition of geographical knowledge (Blaut, McCleary and Blaut, 1970; Blaut and Stea, 1971). Golledge (1981) claims that such work involves 'anchoring of many of the concepts of cognitive mapping in the structuralist theories of Piaget' (p. 1329) but most of it (e.g. the review by Downs and Stea, 1973) pays very little attention to the structuralism arguments and focuses rather on what people know and how they acquire it; it has a strong positivist quality.

It may be that there are other deep structures in human consciousness that are particularly relevant to geographers but are as yet virtually unexplored. An obvious example of this would be the way in which man organizes spatial information and represents it pictorially (and cartographically). Lewis (1981) has recently shown that the ways in which Amerindians organized spatial information were very similar to those proposed by modern geographers, which has led Blouet (1981, p. vi) to wonder:

> to what degree humans are genetically programmed to organise knowledge about the earth's surface in common ways? Are many geographical concepts cross-cultural in the sense that all humans have the capability to generate them as part of their inherited mental equipment, in rather the same way as migratory geese are born with a sense of space that allows them to navigate vast distances by instinct rather than instruments?

The potential for more work in the Piagetian mould is clearly considerable, but as yet relatively little is being done which is truly structuralist, as indicated above.

For the remainder of this chapter, the focus is on 'structure as process', in particular the various forms and derivations of Marxism which have been introduced to human geography in recent years. As Peet (1977) indicates, the adoption of Marxist perspectives grew out of an increasing frustration with the current structure of western society and the inability to achieve major change within it by research in the positivist tradition (see Johnston, 1983a, Chapter 6). This transition is exemplified in the work of David Harvey, one of the major stimulants to the development of Marxist work in geography, who outlines in the introduction to *Social Justice and the City* (1973) the transformation in his own conception of problems and their solutions from an initial 'liberal reform' position (which was positivist; Harvey, 1969) to one based on Marxism, because the latter is holistic, stressing the interdependence of economic and social issues (of production, consumption and distribution).

The introduction of Marxist thought to the main stream of human geography literature in the early 1970s has led to considerable debate over its relevance and to a variety of responses. Several writers have adopted certain aspects of Marxist thought – notably those relating to the economic workings of capitalist society (as in Smith, 1977, 1979) – but without embracing a full Marxist approach. This has been criticized by, for example, Asheim (1979) who argues that such liberal (Marxian rather than Marxist?) formulations fail because: first, they continue to separate production from distribution/consumption, and thus economic from social geography, when Marxist works make it clear that the two are inseparably linked; second, they allocate too much autonomy to the individual as decisionmaker instead of focusing on the constraints of structural relations within the mode of production; and third, they give too much autonomy to the role of space (what is sometimes termed 'spatial fetishism') as a determinant of behaviour, apparently believing that there are immutable 'spatial laws', rather than recognizing that space and spatial relations are part of the structure of the mode of production (space is structured by society, not the other way round).

A full Marxist geography, therefore, is one which accepts the fundamental importance of the organization of production in the creation and structuring of all social processes:

> it is that part of a whole science which specialises in the dialectical relations between social processes on the one hand and the natural environment and spatial relations on the other (Peet and Lyons, 1981, p. 202).

But it is more than a method of analysis, more than a holistic viewpoint based on the primacy of the economic:

> it is aimed at changing the fundamental operation of social processes by changing the social relations of production. Social revolutionary changes are necessary to solve endemic spatial and environmental problems, for these problems originate deep in the capitalist social formations (p. 202).

To Marxists, theory cannot be separated from practice; understanding leds to a programme for change. How Marxist geographers should work to achieve a revolution, from capitalism to socialism, is not made clear by many. The consensus would appear to be the gradualist one suggested by critical theory (see below), whereby appreciation of reality as depicted by Marxist analysis will increase the powers of self-reflection and lead to emancipation from domination. Thus:

> Marxism and Marxist geography provide a powerful theoretical and political base for resistance. They are theories constructed on behalf of the mass of 'ordinary' people of the world to aid in our struggle against an international ruling class and a destructive and exploitative form of social life (Peet and Lyons, 1981, p. 205).

For Harvey (1973), the division of labour within society requires academics to provide the knowledge whereby a revolution in practice is set in motion:

> We are academics . . . As such, our task is to mobilise our powers of thought to formulate concepts and categories, theories and arguments, which we can apply to the task of bringing about a humanizing social change . . . Empirical evidence . . . can and must be used here. But all of those experiences and all of that information means little unless we synthesize it into powerful patterns of thought (p. 145).

His Marxist geography is:

> concerned with the total reconstitution of geographical thought and practices and the ultimate fusion of geographical studies . . . and other subjects under the umbrella of historical materialism (Harvey, 1981, p. 209; see also Eliot Hurst, 1980)

and he argues that:

> geographers inevitably practise politics while politicians just as inevitably engage in geographical practices. Marxists freely acknowledge that link and seek to strengthen rather than hide it (p. 210).

Thus to some, the nature of the holistic perspective of Marxism, as expressed through historical materialism, and of the practical goals of Marxist work means that the division of the social sciences into separate disciplines is counter-revolutionary. Eliot Hurst (1980), for example, argues against any redefinition of human geography. Instead, he argues for a de-definition of all social sciences, replacing them by a single discipline – historical materialism:

> the science of human society ranks alongside mathematical and natural sciences as the only tenable scientific practices (p. 13).

Others disagree, arguing that although the holistic perspective must be retained, the individual social science disciplines are valuable in their provision of particular foci for attention. Dunford (1980), for example, has argued that disciplines can still be identified by their 'distinctive objects' within a historical materialist framework. For human geography, the specific objects of analysis are:

> the spatial forms of human appropriation of nature and of human social organisation (p. 84)

producing the definition that:

> Geography is the study of spatial forms and structures produced historically and specified by modes of production (p. 85).

(The definition is from Scheibling, 1977.) Further, this particular focus has a practical value too. According to Asheim (1979, p. 17):

> The concept of space as the property of the object makes human geography more politically (and practically) relevant, in that the actors become more precisely identified as groups in regional social structures.

The proposition that there is a valid geographical focus within the social sciences is in part related to the concept of structuration. This has been introduced formally to the geographical literature in only a few places (e.g. 'man is obliged to appropriate his material universe in order to survive and . . . he himself has changed through changing the world around him in a continual and reciprocal process'; Gregory, 1978a, p. 89), but is implicitly used by many writers. Within Marxist literature, there is considerable debate between proponents of a 'structure as construct' approach (such as Althusser), who present the economic infrastructure of the mode of production as both dominant and determinant and the elements of the superstructure as dominated and determined (although there is no mention of a deep structure), and proponents of a 'structuralism as process' approach who identify dialectics not only within the infrastructure but also between infrastructure and superstructure. Interpretation of the latter, according to Gregory (1978a, p. 120), means that:

> Spatial structure is not, therefore, merely the area within which class conflicts express themselves . . . but also the domain within which – and, in part, through which – class relations are constituted, and its concepts must have a place in the instruction of the concepts of determinate social formations. (See also Gregory, 1981, p. 11.)

(To Gregory, and others, structuralism implies the 'structure as construct' formulation presented here, so that most interpretations of Marx are not structuralist. A broader definition of structuralism to incorporate 'structure as process' is clearly being advanced here.)

The concept of a dialectic between levels (between superstructure and infrastructure) creates what Soja and Hadjimichalis (1979) term the spatial problematic. Following Lefebvre (see Kurzweil, 1980), they argue that:

112 Structuralist approaches

The class struggle itself is seen as embedded in the structure and contradictions of socially organized space. No social revolution can therefore succeed without being at the same time a spatial revolution (p. 5).

Thus they argue for a need to introduce spatial analysis into Marxist work which, with a few exceptions, displays 'a deep tradition of anti-spatialism' (p. 6). This leads Soja (1980, p. 208) to define a socio-spatial dialectic:

> The structure of organized space is not a separate structure with its own autonomous laws of construction and transformation [this is positivist spatial fetishism], not is it simply an expression of the class structure emerging from the social (i.e. aspatial) relations of production. It represents, instead, a dialectically defined component of the general relations of production relations which are simultaneously social and spacial.

Such a view is represented in a variety of works (e.g. Peet, 1975, on the maintenance of poverty) and provides a clear example of a geographical perspective to Marxist theory. The continuous transformation of capitalism reflects not only the dialectics inherent within the mode of production but also the dialectic between them and their particular spatial realizations. (An outline of research on this theme is given below: p. 114. Note that Eyles, 1981 – quoting Peet – doubts whether the 'spatial dialectics' studied by some Marxist geographers are contradictions in the Marxist sense.)

Human geography is often presented as having a twofold approach: the horizontal, which stresses spatial relationships; and the vertical, which stresses man-environment interrelationships. The latter has also been interpreted in Marxist perspective. Sayer (1979a) has provided a historical materialist discussion of the concept of nature (jointly with the concept of people: 'people and Nature are not separate: we are part of Nature', p. 22) as that which provides the objects of labour (the things worked upon). The transformation of nature is part of the dialectic of the mode of production, according to this view:

> In constructing a building we both transform parts of Nature (sand, wood, stone), objectify human knowledge and reproduce or modify certain social relations (p. 31)

so that:

> in any given historical period the interaction with Nature is locked into a determinate structure of social relations and the eternal necessity of labour (in abstract terms) misleadingly gives the appearance of an eternal necessity of those social relations (p. 32).

Harvey (1974) has illustrated this in another context, showing how conceptions of resources and hence of overpopulation represent a particular conception of nature, that embedded in capitalism. (See also Quaini, 1982, on man's inter-relationships with nature under different modes of production.)

The general theme of all of this work is clearly realist (p. 101) in that it sees the explanation of the phenomena of human geography as lying in hidden mechanisms rather than in the phenomena themselves. Realist philosophy *per se* is explicit in relatively few pieces of geographical writing (e.g. Sayer, 1981), but its tenets provide the implicit foundations for much interpretation. Cox and McCarthy (1982), for example, round out their empirical analyses of the social and spatial correlates of neighbourhood activism in Colombus, Ohio, by presenting such behaviour as an element of false consciousness. It is, they argue, a form of behaviour emanating 'from the structure of social relations in the society as a whole, and not merely from forces unique to the living place' (p. 000), but because most analyses deal only with the observable outcomes of social conflict (the particulars) rather than the determinants (the relations of production) this *real* nature of the behaviour is not revealed. (See also Sayer, 1979b.)

The explication of these hidden mechanisms is the goal of not only a realist philosophy of science (Bhaskar's, 1978, presentation of which includes statements such as 'men must be causal agents capable of acting self-consciously on the world', p. 20, but contains no firm guide as to practice) but also critical theory. This, too, has not been discussed in much of the geographical literature. Lewis and Melville (1975, p. 98) introduced it as:

> recognising the centrality of the relationship between theory and practice by allowing for the effect that knowledge has on those whom it is about . . . a critical theory allows for the fact that hypotheses about society are 'tested' by the development of the class struggle

and this has been developed more fully in Gregory's (1978a) chapter on 'Committed explanation in geography'. To him, the subjects of geographical study must be made more aware of the results of investigations, and indeed be made part of those investigations, through hermeneutic encounters (as in the geographical expeditions in Detroit, Toronto and elsewhere organized by Bunge: Bunge and Bordessa, 1975). But this may compromise the process of self-reflection by focusing it on particulars rather than generalities. Geographers must present:

> (a) a critique of the concepts through which the discipline has sustained its image of the world; and (b) a critique of the processes through which the social formation has sustained its relations of production (p. 165).

(To encourage self-reflection in society as a whole, and to provide the materials for that, geographers must reflect on the nature of their own discipline.) As expressed by Harvey (1973), the task of academics is to develop their powers of analysis, thereby to assist others to develop theirs.

Structuralist geography

Like the humanistic approaches, quite a considerable proportion of the geographical writing in the structuralist mould comprises critique, emphasizing the deficiencies of other approaches (both of those discussed in the two previous chapters). The focus of that critique (as in Massey's, e.g. 1979, of industrial location theory) is that work which is concerned largely with the outcomes of social processes (the locations of industries) and with the impact of individual decision-making (behaviourism) cannot identify the real processes that create and recreate geographies. The retroductive approach, with its focus on the infrastructure, presents an alternative, but this is one which is hard for those accustomed to empirical work to appreciate, because its theories are not testable against empirical evidence in the positivist sense (see p. 99). This is not to argue that empirical work is neither possible nor valuable. Massey and Meegan's (1979) analyses of industrial reorganization illustrate how historical situations influence individual decision-making behaviour but they argue that their findings cannot be generalized away from that specific context. This work is somewhat exceptional, however, in that much 'structure as process' research has forged few links between realist theory and empirical realization. S. Duncan (1981) has illustrated the problems of forging such links, but the theories have provided considerable insights to the study of all aspects of human geography although, as illustrated below, the impact has been greater in some areas of the subject than others.

Economic geography: uneven development A major substantive impact of structuralist work has been on aspects of the geography of development and underdevelopment, transforming this from a subject dominated by ideas relating to a unilinear growth sequence (derived from Rostow's work, see Keeble, 1967) and a deterministic spatial spread of 'modernization' through a country (see Abler, Adams and Gould, 1971) to one thoroughly permeated by, and extending, Marxist political economy. The stimulus for such work comes from the writings of a variety of scholars (for a critical review, see Brewer, 1980; a geographer's review is Brookfield, 1975; see also N. Smith, 1979).

Although the various authorities involved in the study of development differ on the relative importance of certain causative factors, there is general agreement that spatial variations in levels of development between countries are an integral aspect of capitalism:

> the unequal development of regions and nations is as fundamental to capitalism as the direct exploitation of labor by capital (Soja, 1980, p. 219)

is a fundamental axiom of such work. It has been built upon by analyses showing the relationship of imperialism (plus neo-imperialism and neocolonialism) to the accumulation of wealth in certain parts of the world (usually termed the metropolitan cores). One reaction to the falling rate of profit in those areas is to seek cheaper labour and extended markets in other, relatively weak, areas. Thus a thriving core-area bourgeoisie is complemented by an impoverished dependent proletariat in the periphery. At the world scale, this allows a classification, basically of countries, into core and periphery, with an intervening semi-periphery. The core comprises the developed countries and the periphery the underdeveloped or dependent; the former absorb surplus value and the latter export it, with the flows being articulated through the urban system (Johnston, 1980a).

At a finer spatial scale, individual countries can be subdivided into cores, peripheries and semi-peripheries; even the least developed country of the international periphery has its local bourgeoisie concentrated into a certain region, usually a single place (Santos, 1975). Structuralist analyses have shown how such intra-national spatial structures have developed, and have then reproduced themselves, as an example of the socio-spatial dialectic. Again, the emphasis has been on demonstrating the inevitability of such polarization, particularly with the centralization and concentration of the ownership of capital which characterizes recent trends in the transformation of capitalism (Johnston, 1982a).

During the present century, there has been much work in many of the countries at the core of the world economy of what is almost universally known as the 'regional problem'. The major manifestation of this has been (relatively) high unemployment rates in certain regions characterized by a dependence on industries which are in decline. The decline may be a result of a fall of demand for the products or, more likely, a consequence of a shift of investment in those industries to areas where production costs are lower and the potential for accumulation consequently greater (such areas may be in other countries, in some cases several thousand miles from the markets). As with the study of international variations in development, structuralist analysis has sought to relate the regional problem to spatial switches in the pattern of investment, and thus as part of the dialectic between the productive forces and the relations of production. Again, this involves a socio-spatial dialectic. The outcome of one moment of the class struggle in one place (perhaps higher wages for labour, or the implementation of environmental controls: Storper, Walker, and Widess, 1981) can reduce business confidence there and lead to a redirection of investment.

Recently, descriptive analyses in a number of countries (such as the United Kingdom and the United States of America) have identified a new spatial dimension to the pattern of uneven development, the so-called inner-city problem. Initially, it was argued that this reflected deficiencies in the environment of those areas, but later, structuralist-inspired, analyses have argued that the inner cities are merely the latest areas to be deserted by capital as the transformation of the mode of production continues (Thrift, 1979; Hall, 1981a). Thus:

> inherent in capitalist social relations is an unevenness of spatial, political and economic development . . . The emergence of the inner-city problem should be seen in this light. It is not, as such, a new problem in that uneven development has always existed, its novelty lies rather in its promotion to the status of a problem (Forrest et al., 1979, p. 114).

Recognition of this leads the analysts, as in the case of the regional problem, to question the utility and viability of spatial solutions, policies which are area-based in their attempts to boost investment and thereby stimulate employment (Holland, 1976).

As noted above, the articulation of the flows of capital and surplus value takes place through the system of urban places. In addition, of course, the concentration of population into urban places has proved necessary to accommodate the means of production under industrial capitalism. Thus structuralist analyses of urbanization very much follow those of regional variations outlined here, as in Harvey's original analysis of urbanism (Harvey, 1973, Chapter 6; see also Johnston, 1980a, 1982a) and in his later work on capital circuits (Harvey, 1978). Whether the urban area is a sensible focus for analysis – whether there is a specifically urban phenomenon – is, however, a topic of current debate (Saunders, 1981).

All of this work illustrates how uneven economic development and its concomitants, at any scale, are necessary consequences of the processes inherent in capitalism. A framework is provided for understanding such phenomena, and that framework could readily be applied in all aspects of economic geography even though it is not as well developed in some branches (agricultural geography, for example) as others. What is not provided is an explanation for which areas become the cores, and which the peripheries, nor for which areas are likely to decline and which to grow, and so on (Johnston, 1982b). Once the spatial structure is established, the sociospatial dialectic seeks to maintain it. 'Structure as process' provides a *post facto* rationalization for the actual in terms of theories of the real. Because those theories cannot predict how the dialectics will unfold, certainly not in fine spatial detail, they cannot say what will happen where. Realism provides a general understanding within which details about particulars must be fitted.

Social geography: residential segregation As in the work summarized under the previous heading, the introduction of a structuralist approach to social geography, mainly urban social geography, brought about a considerable transformation in research orientations. (Compare, for example, two books on urban residential patterns: Johnston, 1971; Bassett and Short, 1980.) As indicated in Chapter 2 (p. 34), the pre-structuralist work on who lives where within urban areas drew its stimuli from ecology and multivariate statistical analysis. This, it was pointed out (e.g. Eyles, 1974), assumed: first, a given set of social relations; second, no change of a qualitative kind in these relations; third, a consensus within society regarding the 'rightness' of those relations, of the ways in which individuals are allocated to positions within society, and of the ways in which they may seek to change positions; and fourth, free competition for housing, in which all have free choice as to where to live. In effect, it was argued, society is ever-changing (as the relations of production are constantly transformed), is characterized not by consensus but rather by dissensus (and sometimes outright conflict), and contains a variety of mechanisms which constrain both choice of housing and choice of residential area.

These themes were introduced to many social geographers by two of the chapters, on ghetto formation and on urban land-use theory, in Harvey's (1973) *Social Justice and the City*. These set the determinants of land-use patterns not in the abstractions of the 'frictions of distance' nor in the results of free bargaining in choice, but rather in the class relations characteristic of capitalism. Regarding ghettos, Harvey (p. 135) concluded that:

> the rich group can always enforce its preferences over a poor group because it has more resources to apply either to transport costs or to obtaining land in whatever location it chooses.

The explanation for residential separation of socio-economic and other (e.g. racial) groups therefore lies in the infrastructure. Its appearance in the superstructure can be described and modelled, but not accounted for.

Harvey developed his ideas regarding the forces creating residential segregation in a series of general essays plus a detailed study of the housing market in inner Baltimore. In one of the former, he sets out four hypotheses (Harvey, 1975, pp. 362–3):

1 Residential differentiation reflects the reproduction of social relations under capitalism.
2 Residential areas provide milieux within which individuals are socialized.
3 Residential fragmentation into separate communities fragments the class consciousness of the proletariat, thereby hampering the transformation to socialism.
4 Patterns of residential differentiation reflect the contradictions within a class-based society.

From these, he concludes that the creation of urban social areas:

> is produced, in its broad lineaments at least by forces emanating from the capitalist production process and it is not to be construed as the product of the autonomously and spontaneously arising preferences of people (p. 368).

Those preferences are created by the capitalist forces, in the socialization process within community milieux.

Harvey identified a variety of institutions operating with the capitalist economy to assist in the creation of residential separation and thereby to serve the interests of the bourgeoisie and their associates. Analysis of these institutions, the urban gatekeepers and managers, has been the focus of a considerable volume of empirical work (usually termed urban managerialism: Leonard, 1982). Increasingly, however, it was realized that although such work presented useful empirical insights into the workings of housing markets it was not a realist approach in that it focused attention on the decision-makers rather than the context. Thus, stimulated by such works as the translation of Castells' book *The Urban Question* (1977), a more overtly Marxist approach was adopted (e.g. Bassett and Short, 1980).

As in the work on uneven economic development, much of the analysis of the production of residential separation into urban social areas provided rational accounts of why spatial patterns emerge but not of the details of those patterns. Such details are, as pointed out elsewhere in this chapter, irrelevant to the general themes of Marxist work which focus on the major processes rather on the minutiae (trivia?) of how they are realized. Nevertheless, some Marxist analyses of the morphology of social areas have been produced, most notably Walker's (1978, 1981) detailed work on suburbanization in the United States of America, which he associates not only with the desire of the bourgeoisie and their associates to distance themselves from the environmental and social negative externalities of the inner-city but also with the need within capitalist industry to create a demand for 'suburban arcadia'.

Political geography revived A comment by Brian Berry in 1969 that political geography was a 'moribund backwater' (Berry, 1969, p. 450) has been much repeated, both within the small subfield and without. Berry's comment was stimulated by his observation that the 'quantitative revolution' of the 1950s and 1960s made little impact on political geography, which remained a combination of (unrecognized) idealism and pre-positivist empiricism (apart from grand environmentalist theories, such as Mackinder's heartland concept, which was politically unpopular). Despite a major growth in the application of positivist approaches in electoral geography (Taylor and Johnston, 1979), a revival in political geography had to await the stimulus of structuralist approaches.

The conflict focus of the structuralist approaches has provided a number of valuable research themes for political geographers (as illustrated in Burnett and Taylor, 1981; Cox and Johnston, 1982). Many of these centre on the role of the state within capitalist and other modes of production. Until the late 1970s, the nature of the state had not been considered a research problem for political geographers, but work since has tackled the major theoretical issues (e.g. Clark and Dear, 1981; Dear, 1981) and sought to integrate such theory into political geography (Johnston, 1982b). Taylor (198), for example, has used Wallerstein's work on uneven development to provide a materialist framework for political geography.

Historical geography For historical geographers, structuralist approaches offer a realist method of interpreting patterns in the past, just as they do for the economic, social and political geographers of the contemporary scene. Apart from the temporal context, therefore, little may separate them from other branches of geography. If, however, they are interested not in the patterns at one time period but in the processes and patterns of change, then the structuralist approach may be especially appropriate since the changing landscape is presumably a reflection of the dialectics of the mode of production. Thus Gregory (1978b, p. 172) claims that:

> A theory of superstructures cannot, by its very definition, be formulated in exclusively superstructural terms: its examination of discourse must be reciprocally tied to a theory of infrastructures.

Such an approach is particularly valuable for the geographical study of major changes, such as the transformation from feudalism to capitalism (Butlin, 1978) and the subsequent onset of industrialization (Gregory, 1978c), but if one accepts Blaut's (1961) dictum that space is process then it is relevant to all studies of change. (See also Quaini, 1982.)

The process of change, as indicated by the above quotation from Gregory, involves both the dialectics within the infrastructure and the dialectics between superstructure and infrastructure. The role of structuration in the latter has been analysed by Pred using the concepts of time geography. (For similar analyses by non-geographers, see Giddens, 1981; Urry, 1981.) He argues that the impact of technological and institutional innovations involves four 'contrapuntal, or antithetical, dynamics' (Pred, 1978, p. 367):

1 *Individual-societal* – everything that affects an individual affects society, and vice versa.
2 *Daily path-life path* – anything that affects a person's daily activities affects life as a whole, and vice versa.
3 *External-internal* – movements along the daily and life-paths lead to the accumulation of mental experiences, that shape intentions and influence movements.
4 *Path convergence-path divergence* – any new coming-together destroys old paths and any destruction of paths creates new contacts.

The consequences of these conrapuntal dynamics are that:

> the details of social reproduction, individual socialization, and structuration are

constantly spelled out by the intersection of particular paths with particular institutional projects occurring at specific temporal and spatial locations (Pred, 1981a, p. 10).

Pred (1981b) has illustrated this theme with the example of the introduction of factory production, with its consequent disciplines of time (this is the institutional project), and its relationship to family and individual daily life-paths. He showed that time discipline became a necessary part of family life; that the wage-earning male head of household had to be away from the family during much of the day when many important functions had to be performed without him; that wives found themselves further constrained by the discipline of school times; and that free-time projects became increasingly synchronized too. The latter had a noticeable impact on the organization of recreation and sport: the growth of the factory time-discipline led to a particular structuring of the programme of major baseball clubs. (See also his brief biography of his own academic career, Pred, 1979.)

The basic thesis of the 'structure as process' approaches, that the mode of production is continually in transformation as a result of both processes within itself and interaction with the products of earlier transformations, makes it an attractive framework for the study of historical geography. Indeed, it suggests that there is no such thing as historical geography, since change is continuous. The methodology is the same, whatever the time and place of the topic. The data sources and contexts vary, and must be understood by the scholar, but this requirement differs little from the need to understand the spatially-varying cultural contexts of the contemporary world.

Summary

To a considerable extent, a major impact of structuralist works in human geography, as with humanistic, has been as critique. The epistemological and ontological bases of other approaches, notably the positivist, have been laid bare and practitioners have been forced to reflect more on the nature of their work. Thus, as indicated in the next chapter, even if the introduction of the 'structure as process' arguments has not achieved the revolution in geographical practice that some hoped for (e.g. Harvey, 1973, p. 145) it has at least identified some of the problems of the other approaches.

But this is an insufficient achievement, especially for those who argue a strong Marxist line and who see other approaches as counter-revolutionary, both in the sense of the development of understanding and with regard to changing society. To them the only valid epistemology is the realist one: knowledge is obtained not by the accumulation of evidence but by the development of theories which account for the driving forces within society. Such an approach is difficult for many people to accept, because it is not verifiable/falsifiable against evidence in the positivist sense. The test of a theory to a Marxist is not whether it accounts for a certain phenomenon or event but whether it can form the basis for a viable practice, one which will produce change that releases man from domination.

To achieve the Marxist end, especially if this is by the route advanced by critical theorists rather than that of others (not necessarily geographers) which involves revolution and the imposition of a new mode of production, it is necessary for the theories to suggest an acceptable practical route. In the short term, therefore, the work which is done, the theories erected and set against the empirical world, must be interpreted as sensible by others. As illustrated in this chapter, such work is as yet relatively underdeveloped and there are still many topics to be tackled, many debates to be resolved, and many sceptics to be convinced. The contribution so far has involved demonstrating the need for a structuralist approach, indicating that processes must be studied realistically and that the main component of such study is theoretical articulation. To a considerable extent, the actual outcomes of those processes are irrelevant to their understanding. They are relevant, however, to those experiencing the outcomes, whose willingness to accept the structuralist theories may be influenced by their ability to relate outcome and process. In the long-term, the success or failure of the structuralist approaches will depend on the dialectic between theory-producers and 'world residents'.

5
Conflict and accommodation

The previous three chapters have outlined, albeit briefly, the epistemology, ontology, methodology, and substantive contributions of the three approaches which dominate contemporary human geography, in the United Kingdom and North America. Each has been presented separately, with only a few asides to the potential and actual links between them, to the debates between the protagonists for each approach, and to the potential splits within human geography which the existence of three approaches could engender. Clearly, this mode of presentation is to some extent artificial since the development of each approach is in part a function of the contacts and debates between its proponents and those who prefer other philosophies and methodologies. In particular, the humanistic and structuralist approaches have been developed in parallel during the 1970; the research output in both has increased during the decade (thereby providing further evidence against the mono-paradigm model of the history of human geography: Johnston, 1983a) and, as Chapter 2 indicates, activity in the positivist schools has been considerable too.

Despite this somewhat artificial separation, there can be no doubt that the three groups of approaches identified and outlined here do, to a considerable extent, stand alone. This has been made clear, for example, in a discussion of the use of metaphors in the development of geographical knowledge. Harrison and Livingstone (1982) point out that each of the three approaches has its own particular metaphors. For the positivist approaches (they term them functionalist) these are machine and organism, implying a well-structured system regulated to operate and to evolve in a particular way; physical science and engineering are the main sources of relevant analogies. For the humanistic approaches (their term is subjectivism) the identified metaphors are text and language game, indicating the focus on thoughts, words, and actions. Finally, for the structuralist perspective they identify construction and domination as the relevant metaphors; construction implies that the constituting structures have to be created by the theorist, because they cannot be identified by observation, whereas that of domination represents the basic feature of the societies being represented in the structures.

Can these metaphors, and the approaches that they represent, be accommodated in a single, pluralistic approach to human geography, or must they remain the possession of separate, irreconcilable approaches? As reviewed elsewhere (Johnston, 1983a), there has been considerable debate over this issue during recent years, some of it relatively vituperative. The purpose of this concluding chapter is not to provide a further detailed review of those debates. Instead the focus is on the central issue: three (or more) geographies or one?

Three geographies?

A great deal of academic debate (like any other) polarizes opinion, in part because of the opposition between the points of view and in part because, as Harvey (1973, p. 128) candidly recognizes, presentation of one's views as both original and superior is a common tactic in seeking to advance an academic career. The result of the debate can be one of several positions, and individuals may differ in which they choose to take. Thus the debate may be inconclusive, in that neither side converts the other, in which case the consequence may be either studied ignorance of each other's positions or continued attempts to win converts. One side may win, however, in which case adherents of the losing position change their opinions and adopt those of their victors (i.e. those who have 'proved' that they have the better answer to the problems under discussion); it is quite common, incidentally, for the 'vanquished' to retain some of the characteristics of their earlier beliefs. Or the proponents of each side accept that they have polarized the situation too far; each realizes that the other's arguments have some merit, and an attempt is made to forge an accommodation incorporating the best of both.

Aspects of all of these results can be found in the geographical literature. Some converts have clearly been made (e.g. Harvey, 1973; see also the essays in Billinge, Gregory and Martin, 1982). Some recognize the validity of other approaches but prefer to distance themselves from them; much debate continues. And some people are seeking accommodations. It would be difficult to assess who is winning, or what the criteria for victory are.

Such debate is not new to human geography, of course. It has characterized its entire academic history, as numerous published debates and reviews make clear. In the 1950s and 1960s, for example, adherents of the positivist approaches criticized the empiricists/exceptionalists for 'mere description', and in return were taken to task for 'using a statistical sledgehammer to crack a nut' and 'spatial determinism'. And, of course, similar debates rage in the other social sciences (an excellent review, slanted towards the structural approach, is provided by Keat and Urry, 1975; see also Keat, 1981; Hindess, 1977). Indeed, since the stimuli for philosophical and methodological changes in human geography have come almost entirely from explorations of the literature of other disciplines, it is not surprising that the discipline has been far from immune from the general debates with social science.

Associated with much of the debate over the relevance of the various approaches, in the social sciences in general and in human geography in particular, is ideology. Most authors who discuss this concept in any detail stress its complexity and the great variety of ways in which it is used. Nevertheless, Keat and Urry (1975, p. 176) feel able to identify the common elements in the various usages as:

> the term is applied to sets of beliefs, or concepts, or theories, and is normally derogatory or pejorative. In particular, in the social sciences, to refer to a theory as ideological involves the claim that theory is in some way distorted. It fails to meet appropriate criteria of knowledge or validity, and is to that extent objectionable or mistaken.

Larrain (1979) does not disagree, but suggests that two types of ideology can be identified. The negative type uses ideology:

> as a critical concept which means a form of false consciousness or necessary deception which somehow distorts men's understanding of social reality (pp. 13-14)

whereas the positive type uses ideology as:

> the expression of the world-view of a class . . . the opinions, theories and attitudes formed within a class in order to defend and promote its interests (p. 14).

The (often implicit) existence of such ideologies is apparent in the debates within human geography, especially those between positivists on the one hand and realists/critical theorists on the other.

Into battle

Given that positivist approaches were firmly established in human geography (as in most other social sciences) prior to the other two discussed here, much of the debate has been aimed at positivism although, reflecting the contemporaneity of all three, some statements favouring one approach condemn both of the others. Thus Ley and Samuels (1976) promote humanistic approaches in a critique of positivist approaches as 'dehumanizing' and 'reductionist', and Ley (1978) attacks Marxism (basically Althusserian Marxism it seems) as:

> a world of reductionism, a world of pallid human profiles where the moves of the faceless and mindless ones are determined according to the system of an outside operator . . . Materialism, reductionism, determinism; these are the characteristics of an epistemology and an ideology of manipulation that has a unauthentic model of man (p. 48).

Regarding the humanistic approaches, positivists are critical because of their subjectivity and idiographic nature (which reflects on the relative weak development of the basic goals of phenomenology within the geographical literature), but the antagonisms are not great. Indeed, behavioural positivist work has been influenced by the humanistic approaches. Among structuralists, on the other hand, the humanistic approaches are condemned because they give man complete freedom of action (within the constraints of an – apparently unrecognized – pure consciousness) rather than realize the degree to which the limits to human thought and action are imposed by the infrastructure. Rieser (1973) calls this humanistic approach psychologism, which contradicts Marx's statement that 'men make their own history, but not in circumstances of their own choosing'; individuals' meanings use a socialized language.

The structuralist critique of work in the positivist mould focuses on the (frequently implicit) assumptions that its generalizations have a timeless quality; they are a first approximation of universal laws (see Gregory, 1978a, for one of the fullest critiques). Thus Sayer (1979a) claims that:

> positivist science, such as locational analysis, expects to find invariant, universal empirical regularities of human behaviour. Any regularities discovered at a particular point in time are hopefully expected to hold true for the future while repeated failures to corroborate such regularities are treated as failures of the individual scientist or model, rather than as evidence of qualitative selfchange of history (p. 30).

Such a naturalistic perspective is wrong for the social sciences, he claims, because realism differs between the physical and social sciences:

> Whereas we can control Nature only by obeying its laws, we can change the very terms of social laws, by *changing* them.

The critique of positivism extends to its use – both proposed and intended. This, as discussed in Chapter 2, is sometimes known as instrumentalism – use of the predictive ability of a theory: 'Theories are instruments, and, as such, only their utility can be assessed, and not their truth or falsity. They do not provide any knowledge . . . over and above the predictions that can be derived from them' (Keat and Urry, 1975, p. 63). Gregory (1980) illustrates this in a critique of work (especially that of Bennett and Chorley, 1978) on systems theory, which he indicates is concerned with control and regulation and therefore with maintenance of the status quo. Positivist work is used to ensure the reproduction of the existing structure of society, rather than to allow it to evolve dialectically.

The responses to such attacks on positivist approaches usually focus on the tentative nature of structuralist, especially realist, theories and the nature of the retroductive methodology. Thus in a review of a structuralist volume (Dear and Scott, 1981), Hall (1981b) expresses his frustrations with Marxist urban studies, marked in the 1970s by:

an almost obsessive concern with theory construction and a tendency to shunt off for the future the tedious job of empirical justification. One would expect, after a decade of work, a marriage of the theory with a strong empirical tradition . . . [But Marxists] appear content to work with generalisations of a very loose kind, in which temporal association itself constitutes proof of causation (pp. 439-440).

Hall clearly wishes to apply positivist criteria to structuralist theory, despite the arguments (see p. 99) that the unique characteristics of every moment in a dialectic prevent any development of generalizations. To Chisholm, the introduction of Marxism to human geography represents a 'misconceived counter-revolution':

> Harvey wants us to embrace the Marxist 'method' of dialectic. This 'method' passes my understanding; so far as it has a value, it seems to be as a metaphysical belief system and not – as its protagonists proclaim – a mode of rational argument (Chisholm, 1975, p. 175).

And finally, to Muir (1978) Marxism (again, vulgar Marxism it seems: Duncan, 1979b) is a rigid doctrine within which no dissent is allowed. Those who have put Marxism into action in Eastern Europe are the ones against whom the validity of the method must be judged (although as a predictive tool Marxism 'is simply wrong)'; It is characterized by:

> the commands from such little men as Marx, Lenin, Trotsky, Stalin and Mao concerning the primacy of activism, the obligations of party membership and the necessity to subordinate individual judgement to the will of the party (Muir, 1979, p. 126).

In all of these critiques and debates, ideology is a relevant factor – although often hidden. Structuralists, especially critical theorists, have a clear positive ideology, a world-view of a society in which man is dominated at present because of alienation and of a society in the future in which such domination and alienation are removed. Thus to Sayer (1979b), for example, an adequate theory for urban planning is not only integrated into a wider theory of society (the present world view) but must 'take account of its own effect in changing its object of study' (p. 861; the future world view). The negative ideologies identified are both mystifications. That provided by the humanistic approaches offers a false view of man in that it presents him as master of himself rather than as a dominated person. That provided by the positivist approaches suggests that man can create a better world for himself (scientific politics, p. 13) without realizing that he will be dominated in that world too.

Others, too, have ideological bases to their critiques, as in the negative ideology of positivism presented by Powell (1980). Ley's critique of 'the loss of the geographic subject' in both positivism and Marxism (in the latter men are 'puppets') reflects his ideological fears:

Conceptual reductionism might well give rise to an existential reductionism, as men may actually assume the role of the uncomplimentary puppets that the state's theorists model and its social engineers plan for. In such a setting . . . ethical and moral issues are themselves appropriated into the domain of the technical . . . even the expression of such basic human freedoms as free speech, free assembly and freedom to worship may be disqualified as incompatible with rational systems of control (Ley, 1980, p. 19).

Finally, as an example of the positive ideology of positivists, Abler, Adams and Gould (1971) argue that:

> Like it or not, geography and the other social sciences have pressing social and moral responsibilities. We see no alternative to practising geography as a science if we hope to meet these obligations (p. 21).

And:

> explanation and manipulation are the focus of our discipline today and will continue to be in the future. Because of our wish to manipulate events, we must explain both process and structure to ourselves so we can intervene in process to produce the spatial structure of activities we desire (p. 88).

Accommodation

The series of statements quoted above suggests little ground for any accommodation between the proponents of the different approaches. And yet the polarized positions illustrated there are, not unsurprisingly, somewhat extreme and closer inspection reveals some interpenetration of the approaches. Indeed, some of them have the same basic ends; for example, both transcendental phenomenology and 'structure as construct' structuralism are seeking 'pure consciousness' or its equivalent but by very different methods, and there has been discussion of the development of a phenomenological Marxism (Smart, 1976). And, even more importantly with regard to the content of contemporary human geography, critical theory is built on a combination of hermeneutics and Marxist political economy.

Some authors are prepared to concede to other approaches than their own by arguing that they are complementary: there is more than one mode of analysis necessary to appreciate all aspects of society. Thus Tuan (1977, p. 5) accepts that:

> we measure and map space and place, and acquire spatial laws and resource inventories for our efforts. These are important approaches, but they need to be complemented by experiential data that we can collect and interpret in measured confidence because we are human ourselves.

This suggests a fragmentation of the discipline, or at least a lack of any desire to put the various approaches together; they simply coexist. Others grudgingly allow elements of one approach within their own, but only in a subordinate role. Walker (1981b), for example:

> does not demand wholesale rejection of statistical manipulation, which is, after all, still a useful tool for sorting and arranging data and eliminating egregiously misguided generalizations (p. 8).

But he rejects the scientific view of 'natural law' and a natural social order which cannot be altered by social practice. (The latter also suggests rejection of phenomenology, with its belief in ultimate knowledge which is independent of man.)

Finally, there are those, most of them inclined to the positivist approaches, who accept some of the arguments for the alternatives but wish to retain at least part of their former position. King (1979), for example, acknowledges that some of the quantitative-theoretical work may have been misdirected, but can still 'acknowledge readily that it represents scholarship of the highest order' (King, 1976, p. 157). What he seeks is a middle course. He claims that:

> As with any approach, the prescriptions based upon the Marxist interpretations are palatable only to those who accept the ideological frameworks within which they are set. It would seem foolish, however, . . . to ignore the approach (p. 306).

They are obviously unpalatable to him. He wishes to work within the present structure of society. Regarding his own work on unemployment he asks:

> What is the basis of my judgement that unemployment is bad? Certainly it does not lie in any profound Christian belief in the virtue of labor, nor can I be convinced that 'unemployed' persons drawing government insurance benefits are less happy than I am, but I do know that the costs of such programs are a charge to me as a taxpayer, and I reject this form of equalization policy (p. 303).

To reduce his taxes, 'One of my more important premises is that social science must contribute to social policy and the shaping of social change' (p. 302). His middle course, 'between the straits of pure positivism and scientific socialism', is outlined to that end, and involves the researcher using metaphors and other storytelling techniques to inform and lead policy-makers. Thus King, like many others, has revised his position within the positivist approaches as a result of contact with the structuralist, but has not been convinced of any need to alter his basis epistemological stance; he remains, it seems, a logical positivist.

Integration?

The discussion in the previous section has intimated that although some human geographers have been prepared to accept certain elements of other approaches, most have remined firmly entrenched in one approach only and have used the negative concept of ideology (often referred to as values, Sayer, 1981) to criticize what are seen as competing philosophies. Few have explored the potential for integrating the various approaches, or at least elements of them.

Such an exploration was attempted by Hay (1979), in an essay intended largely as a defence of the positivist approaches against both humanistic and structuralist critiques but in a constructive rather than a destructive manner. The defence of positivism is phrased largely in terms of the four definitions later provided by Keat (1981; p. 13). In effect, Hay rejects scientism, scientific politics, and value-freedom, and argues only for the 'positivist conception of science' as a viable mode of study in certain circumstances. He concludes that:

> the question to be asked of a geographic theory is not 'does this theory *totally* explain the observed variation?' but the more modest question, 'does this theory contribute an explanation of a part of the observed variation which would otherwise remain obscure? If the claims of location theory are couched in these terms the critique ceases to be important (p. 9).

He then reviews the humanistic and structuralist approaches, which might provide explanations of other parts of the observed variation, and decides that together the three approaches:

> allow within human geography at the same time a *nomological* geography which seeks, for example, to understand the workings of urban rent theory as positivistically observed, a *hermeneutic* geography which seeks to identify the meaning of the urban rent system for those who are participants (active or passive) within it, and a *critical* geography which points to the extent to which present urban rent systems are themselves transformations of the capitalist system, but which admits that some of its features may indeed by 'invariant regularities' (p. 22).

Such a reconciliation of the three approaches clearly allocates primacy to the positivist. Somewhat similarly, Livingstone and Harrison (1981, p. 370) argue a humanistically-focused reconciliation:

> a humanistic geography which is, at the same time, *critical*, in questioning rather than bracketing our presuppositions, *hermeneutic*, in interpreting the meanings behind action, and *empirical*, in examining the subjectively interpreted objective world.

Hay's attempt at a reconciliation of the three approaches contained an implicit definition of human geography as a naïve realist discipline, one concerned with positive research in an empirical fashion. In structuralist terms, the major concerns of his human geography reside in the superstructure. Such a definition was made explicit by Johnston (1980b, 1982c), who also sought some integration of the three approaches. He, too, rejected many of the broader conceptions of positivism, seeing its quantitative tools only as a valid way to achieve descriptive generalizations. His argument was that explanation and/or understanding (answers to the question 'why?') could not be achieved within the positivist approach. The structuralist provides the basic understanding of economic, social and political processes, and certain humanistic approaches (notably idealism) offer the greatest potential for accounting for the decision-making processes leading to particular realizations of those processes. Thus a naïve realist discipline, concerned with the spatial morphology of the superstructure, needs more than a structuralist approach.

Other authors have claimed that such accommodations and reconciliations between the various approaches are unfeasible. Eyles and Lee (1982), for example, suggest that eclectic abstraction of elements of different approaches is not possible because those approaches are founded not on methodological or analytical bases but on epistemological differences. One cannot, they argue, integrate a humanistic with a positivist approach because they have independent conceptions of knowledge. Nevertheless, Eyles (1981) has argued for an integration of Marxist with humanistic approaches, to allow for individuality and experiences (the everyday ones analysed by Schutz: see p. 62) which are 'meaningful in their own right' (p. 1382); Eyles believes that 'no geography . . . can be complete without Marxism' (p. 1336) but that this alone is insufficient for the study and improvement of lived experience. On different grounds Silk (1982) advances the ideological argument that such electicism 'serves the bourgeoisie well' in maintaining the status quo. Finally, Gregory (1978a, p. 169) argues that:

> inchoate eclecticism, however comforting it might appear, is no solution because . . . all conceptions of critical science require an effort of their practitioners which obliges them to articulate the bases of (the interests in) their own practical activities . . . If we speak about residential differentiation for example, we need to clarify the status of concepts like 'class' and 'rent' and to recognize their essentially and intrinsically political connotations.

The arguments will undoubtedly continue, if for no other reason than that many (most?) human geographers feel unable to accept the content of the last phrase in the above quotation. Both positivist and humanistic approaches have something in common with their conceptions of value-freedom and bracketing, which are contrary to the theory as practice foundation of critical science. And many too, as Berry (1973) has made clear in a number of his statements on spatial planning, are not attracted to notions of revolutionary political change.

One of the as yet unresolved issues in this debate, raised by Johnston (1980b), concerns the scale of analysis, in particular the time scale but not only so. As made clear in the discussion in Chapter 5 of the historical materialist approach, Marx was basically interested in the general course of history rather than with the particulars of certain events. For this reason, he held that no individual, however powerful and important he or she might seem at the time, could alter the course of history (instead 'cometh the hour . . .'). Most historians, however, are interested in particular events, in which the roles of individuals may be crucial. For human geographers, it was also shown in Chapter 5 that much of the theory-writing in the 'structuralism as process' school is concerned with broad patterns, of economic development for example, rather than with the detailed delineation of what is where, and why. Again, it can be argued that individuals are not relevant to the unfolding of the general pattern, but if geographers are interested in particulars within that, then the use of quantitative approaches to manipulate data and of humanistic approaches to understand relevant decisions may be justified. Thus, it is argued, human geographers interested in the details of space and place may operate within the context of a 'structure as process' theory; they may consider themselves allied with the critical science position by seeking to achieve realist ends by linking theory to outcome, and they may use elements of the other approaches to achieve those links (see Johnston, 1982b).

Little work has been done which explicitly demonstrates how the various approaches might be integrated. That which has been done focuses on the structuralist and humanistic approaches, which have the most points of contact. Positivism is much harder to integrate with the others, because of its emphases on objectivity and empirical generalizations and its belief that explanations can be identified in the empirical phenomena themselves; the last is illustrated by the emphasis on distance as a causal variable in spatial science. (Note, however, that quantification should not be associated solely with positivism, as both Taylor, 1981, and Walker, 1981b, make clear. As a means of manipulating information, quantification can be employed within any social scientific philosophy. It is associated with positivism through its use to infer and to make generalizations and laws. It can be associated with humanistic and structuralist work as a descriptive tool, although some – e.g. Sayer, 1979a – doubt that this is needed very much.)

Attempts to integrate structuralist and humanistic approaches focus on the decision-making activities of individuals within structural imperatives. They develop on, or are related to, the work on structuration, as illustrated (p. 119) by Pred's analyses of structural influences on the organization of time and space. The structural imperative is provided by the ongoing economic processes within the mode of production. The humanistic input focuses on actions taking place at the superstructural level within those processes. The latter is needed for an empirical discipline, one which is concerned not only with the general processes within the infrastructure but also with the particular outputs. To use a sporting analogy, an empirical discipline seeks to account for both the rules of the game and the outcome of an individual match. Human geography, many argue, is such an empirical discipline.

The revived subdiscipline of political geography provides examples of attempts to combine humanistic and structuralist perspectives. (It also illustrates – e.g. Archer and Taylor, 1981 – the use of quantitative analyses in a non-positivist context.) The structuralist perspective is provided by analyses of the materialist base of the capitalist world economy (Taylor, 1982). This, to use Giddens' (1979) terminology, is both enabling and constraining. It is enabling in that it creates the environment for human action, but constraining in that it restricts the range of action to decisions that mesh with the imperatives of the structural process. Maintenance of the materialist base requires a supportive set of institutions. No particular type of institution is necessary. All that is needed is a form which both legitimizes the mode of production (the capitalist world economy) and facilitates success in its strategy of wealth accumulation. The institution that has been created to undertake these tasks is the state, which has a territorial definition and so is a geographical entity. Such an institution was not necessary, because the situation was an enabling one in which another mode of organization could have been developed; but it was sufficient.

Political geography, then, requires a theory of the state, of its role within the capitalist world economy (Johnston, 1980c). But for an empirical discipline this is insufficient. The economic forces driving the system require the state to provide both legitimation and a conducive environment for accumulation, but they do not demand that it make a particular decision on each issue. Within the constraints set by the twin needs of legitimation and accumulation, there is some freedom of decision-making allowed: a British government may be constrained to adopt policies that will reduce costs for employers, but it may choose to do this in a variety of ways – employment subsidies, perhaps, or incomes policies and restraints on the activities of trade unions.

Within the theory of the state, therefore, the empirical discipline of political geography needs a methodology for understanding state actions. This requires a focus on the actors involved – politicians, bureaucrats, and, where relevant, electors and pressure groups. (For an extended discussion of this, see Johnston, 1982b.) The role of politicians in the allocation of public money to different parts of a state's territory (Johnston, 1980d), the work of bureaucratic managers in the control of access to housing (Leonard, 1982;

Williams, 1982), and the decisions of judges on cases relating to the organization of space (Johnston, 1981c) – all illustrate this need to understand how individuals act within the state; a recent paper has presented possible methodology for such work (Johnston, 1983b). And where large numbers of actors are involved, as in the casting of votes, quantitative procedures can be employed to display the geographical consequences of 'manipulation in the material base of . . . society' (Archer and Taylor, 1981, p. x).

The purpose of the integration, therefore, is to illustrate how general processes, such as that of urbanization (Johnston, 1980a), produce different patterns of spatial organization because they encounter particular historical, cultural, and environmental situations (Johnston, 1982a). It is not, however, without its problems, particularly for those in the 'Marxism as practice' school of thought. Taylor (1983) has identified three types of political geographers: status quo empiricists; liberal reformers, who espouse positions like that described in the previous paragraph; and radicals. But, he argues, there are only two possible positions for these groups to occupy, with the liberal reformers as the 'odd group out':

> Their efforts to combine the incompatible may be seen as a brave attempt to generate a viable alternative to the status quo and radical positions. It has been unsuccessful because there can be only two types of theory: traditional and critical. The former support the status quo, the latter expose it as part of a process of overthrowing it (Taylor, 1983)

Johnston (1983c) has responded with a defence of the academic position of the 'liberal reformers'. But he has to admit that personal 'revolutionary' or 'reformist' aims may be thwarted in the use to which research results are put. Research in the critical theory context may be used in a counter-revolutionary rather than the desired revolutionary way to support the status quo in society (the terms are taken from Harvey, 1973) because of some failure in the hermeneutic component (see p. 61). The human geographer cannot be sure that his or her work will be interpreted in the way that he wishes it to be, if he or she accepts that social change must be achieved by argument, not force.

The integration of structuralist and humanistic perspectives allows the study of particular empirical topics to be set in a proper context, therefore, according to some arguments. As such, understanding should be enriched. But the point made by Gregory (p. 130 above) regarding political connotations and practices is a vital one. Is the human geographer outlined in the previous paragraph presenting a valuefree, suppositionless position? Is he or she committed to the maintenance of the status quo politically? If the answer to the second question is 'yes', then the position is logical and can be defended and attacked. If, however, the answer to the first question is 'yes', the problem is raised regarding the utility of the work. The researcher may present the results of research in an 'objective and politically neutral manners. But he or she cannot ensure that those results either remain as 'pure research' or are not treated in a way designed to achieve a particular political goal. Applied research is directed to a particular end. Applicable research is the use of one person's work for another's ends, and the original researcher cannot control the usage, unless the results of the work are kept secret. Thus the researcher working within the (implicit or explicit) context described above is in a dilemma: the research may be used for instrumentalist purposes (see p. 44), by powerful elements within society with whom the researcher may have little sympathy.

Conclusion

This book has ended with a dilemma, deliberately so, because human geographers face a dilemma at the present time. (Indeed they undoubtedly always have, but it is probably more obvious now.) They must either choose between a variety of approaches to human geography or seek to fashion a middle course incorporating elements of two or more of those approaches. Further, they must choose in the knowledge that the concepts of value-freedom and objectivity in social science are under increasing challenge, as it is demonstrated that theory and practice are inseparably linked. Their choice has political as well as academic connotations, which they cannot avoid. The present discussion has outlined the material that must be used in making that choice but no attempt has been made to suggest what it should be, though undoubtedly hints of a personal view will have come through.

Bibliography

Abler, R. F., Adams, J. S. and Gould, P. R. 1971: *Spatial organization*. Englewood Cliffs: Prentice-Hall.
Agnew, J. A. and Duncan, J. S. 1981: The transfer of ideas into Anglo-American human geography. *Progress in Human Geography* **5**, 42-57.
Amedeo, D. and Golledge, R. G. 1975: *An introduction to scientific reasoning in geography*. New York: John Wiley.
Andreski, S. (ed.) 1974: *The essential Comte*. London: Croom Helm.
Appleton, J. 1975: *The experience of landscape*. Chichester: John Wiley.
Archer, J. C. and Taylor, P. J. 1981: *Section and party*. Chichester: John Wiley.
Ardrey, R. 1969 *The territorial imperative*. London: Fontana.
Asheim, B. T. 1979: Social geography – welfare state ideology or critical social science? *Geoforum* **10**, 5-18.
Ayer, A. J. 1964: *Language, truth and logic*. Second edition. London: Victor Gollancz.
Ballabon, M. B. 1957: Putting the 'economic' into economic geography. *Economic Geography* **33**, 217-223.
Barnes, B. 1982: *T. S. Kuhn and social science*. London: Macmillan.
Bassett, K and Short, J. R. 1980: *Housing and residential structure*. London: Routledge and Kegan Paul.
Bauman, Z. 1978: *Hermeneutics and social science*. London: Hutchinson.
Beavon, K. S. O. 1976: *Central place theory*. London: Longman.
Bennett, R. J. 1979a: Space-time models and urban geographical research. In D. T. Herbert and R. J. Johnston(eds.), *Geography and the urban environment*. Volume 2 (Chichester: John Wiley).27-58.
—— 1979b: *Spatial time series*. London: Pion.
—— 1980: *The geography of public finance*. London: Methuen.
—— 1981a: Quantitative and theoretical geography in Western Europe. In R.J. Bennett (ed.) *European Progress in Spatial Analysis*. (London: Pion) 1-34.
—— 1981b: A hierarchical control solution to allocation of the British Rate Support Grant. *Geographical Analysis* **13**, 300-314.
—— and Chorley, R. J. 1978: *Environmental systems: philosophy, analysis and control*. London: Methuen.
—— and Wrigley, N. 1981: Introduction, quantitative and theoretical geography: retrospect and prospect. In N. Wrigley and R. J. Bennett (eds.): *Quantitative geography in Britain: retrospect and prospect*, 3-11. London: Routledge and Kegan Paul.
Berry, B. J. L. 1969: Book review *Geographical Review* **59**, 450.
—— 1973: *The human consequences of urbanization*. London: Macmillan.
—— and Horton, F. E. (eds.) 1970: *Geographic perspectives on urban systems*. Englewood Cliffs: Prentice-Hall.
Bhaskar, R. 1975: *A realist theory of science*. Brighton: Harvester Press.

Bibliography

—— 1979: *The possibility of naturalism*. Brighton: Harvester Press.
Billinge, M. 1977: In search of negativism: phenomenology and historical geography. *Journal of Historical Geography* 3, 55–67.
——, Gregory, D. and Martin, R. L. (eds.) 1982: *Reflections on a revolution*. London: Macmillan.
Blakemore, M. J. 1981: From way-finding to map-making. *Progress in Human Geography* 5, 1–24.
Blaut, J. M. 1961: Space and process. *The Professional Geographer* 13(4), 1–7.
——, McCleary, G. and Blaut, A. S. 1970: Environmental mapping in young children. *Environment and Behavior* 2, 335–349.
Blaut, J. M. and Stea, D. 1971: Studies of geographic learning *Annals, Association of American Geographers* 61, 387–393.
Blouet, B. W. 1981: Preface in B. W. Blouet (ed.); *The origins of academic geography in the United States* (Hamden, Conn.: Archon Books.)
Boden, M. A. 1979: *Piaget*. London: Fontana.
Bottomore, T. 1978: Marxism and sociology. In Bottomore, T. and Nisbet, R. (eds.): *A history of sociological analysis*. (London: Heinemann), 118–148.
Braithwaite, R. B. 1953: *Scientific explanation*. Cambridge: Cambridge University Press.
Breitbart, M. M. 1981: Peter Kropotkin, the anarchist geographer In Stoddart, D. R. (ed.): *Geography, ideology and social concern*. (Oxford: Basil Blackwell), 134–153.
Brewer, A. 1980: *Marxist theories of imperialism*. London: Routledge and Kegan Paul.
Brookfield, H. C. 1975: *Interdependent development*. London: Methuen.
Brown, R. H. 1943: *Mirror for Americans: likeness of the Eastern Seaboard 1810*. New York: American Geographical Society.
Bunting, T. E. and Guelke, L. 1979: Behavioral and perception geography: a critical appraisal. *Annals, Association of American Geographers* 69, 448–462.
Burnett, A. D. and Taylor, P. J., (eds.) 1981: *Political studies from spatial perspective*. Chichester: John Wiley.
Burton, I. 1963: The quantitative revolution and theoretical geography. *The Canadian Geographer* 7, 151–162.
Butlin, R. A. 1978: The late middle ages c. 1350–1500. In Dodgshon, R. A. and Butlin, R. A., (eds.): *An historical geography of England and Wales* (London: Academic Press) 199–149.
Buttimer, A. 1979: Erewhon or nowhere land. In Gale, S. and Olsson, G. (eds.): *Philosophy in geography* (Dordrecht: D. Reidel), 9–37.
Buttimer, A. 1981: On people, paradigms and 'progress' in geography. In Stoddart, D. R. (ed.): *Geography, ideology and social concern*. (Oxford: Basil Blackwell) 81–99.
Carlstein, T. 1980: *Time, resources, society and ecology*. Lund: Department of Geography, Royal University of Lund.
Caro, R. A. 1975: *The power broker: Robert Moses and the fall of New York*. New York: Vintage Books.
Castells, M. 1977: *The Urban Question*. London: Edward Arnold.
Chapman, G. P. 1977 *Human and environmental systems*. London: Academic Press.
Chisholm, M. 1967: General systems theory and geography. *Transactions, Institute of British Geographers* 42, 45–52.
—— 1975 *Human geography: evolution or revolution?* London: Penguin.
—— 1979: *Rural settlement and land use*. London: Hutchinson.
Chorley, R. J. 1964: Geography and analogue theory. *Annals of the Association of*

American Geographers **54**, 127–137.
Chorley, R. J. 1973: Geography as human ecology. In R. J. Chorley (ed.): *Directions in geography* (London: Methuen), 155–170.
——and Haggett, P. (eds.) 1967: *Models in geography*. London: Methuen.
Clark, G. L. and Dear, M. 1981 The state in capitalism and the capitalist state. In Dear, M. J. and Scott A. J. (eds.), *Urbanization and urban planning in capitalist society* (London: Methuen), 45–62.
Cliff, A. D. and Ord, J. K. 1980: *Spatial processes*. London: Pion.
Cliff, A. D. et al 1981: *Spatial diffusion*. Cambridge: Cambridge University Press.
Collingwood, R. G. 1946: *The idea of history*. Oxford: Oxford University Press.
——1965: *Essays in the philosophy of history*. Austin: University of Texas Press.
Cox, K. R. 1976: American geography: social science emergent. *Social Science Quarterly* **57**, 182–207.
——1981: Bourgeois thought and the behavioral geography debate. In Cox, K.R. and Golledge, R.G. (eds.), *Behavioral problems in geography revisited* (London: Methuen), 256–280.
——and Johnston, R. J. editors 1982: *Conflict, politics and the urban scene*. London: Longman.
——and McCarthy, J. J. 1982 Neighbourhood activism as a politics of turf. In Cox, K. R. and Johnston, R. J. (eds.), *Conflict, politics and the urban scene* (London: Longman), 196–218.
Cybriwsky, R. and Ley, D. 1974: Urban graffiti as territorial markers. *Annals, Association of American Geographers* **64**, 491–505.
Dear, M. J. (1981) The state: a research agenda. *Environment and Planning A*. **13**, 1191–96.
Dear, M. J. and Scott, A. J. (eds.) 1981: *Urbanization and urban planning in capitalist society*. London: Methuen.
Downs, R. M. and Stea, D. 1973: Cognitive maps and spatial behavior: process and products. In R. M. Downs and D. Stea, (eds.) *Image and environment* (London: Edward Arnold), 8–26.
——1977: *Maps in minds*. New York: Harper and Row.
Duncan, J. S. 1981: From container of women to status symbol: the impact of social structure on the meaning of the house. In Duncan, J. S. (eds.) *Housing and identity* (Beckenham: Croom Helm), 36–59.
Duncan, S. S. 1979a Qualitative change in human geography – an introduction. *Geoforum* **10**, 1–5.
——1979b: Radical geography and Marxism. *Area* **11**, 124–126.
——1981: Housing policy, the methodology of levels, and urban research: the case of Castells. *International Journal of Urban and Regional Research* **5**, 231–254.
Dunford, M. 1980: *Historical materialism and geography*. Brighton: University of Sussex, Research Papers in Geography.
Eliot Hurst, M. E. 1980: Geography, social science and society: towards a de-definition. *Australian Geographical Studies* **18**, 3–21.
Entrikin, J. N. 1976: Contemporary humanism in geography. *Annals, Association of American Geographers* **66**, 615–632.
Ewing, A. C. 1934: *Idealism: a critical survey*. London: Methuen.
Eyles, J. 1974: Social theory and social geography. In Board, C. et al., (eds.) *Progress in geography* **6**, (London: Edward Arnold), 27–88.
Eyles, J. 1981: Why geography cannot be Marxist: towards an understanding of lived experience. *Environment and Planning A* **13**, 1371–1388.
——and Lee, R. 1982: Human geography in explanation. *Transactions, Institute of*

British Geographers **NS7**, 117-122.
Farber, M. 1943: *The foundation of phenomenology*. Cambridge, Mass.: Harvard University Press.
Flew, A. 1975: *Thinking about thinking*. London: Fontana.
Forrest, R. et al. 1979: The inner city: in search of the problem. *Geoforum* **10**, 109-116.
Freeman, T. W. 1961 *A hundred years of geography*. London: G. Duckworth.
—— 1980: *A history of modern British geography*. London: Longman.
Garfinkel, H. 1967: *Studies in ethnomethodology*. Englewood Cliffs: Prentice-Hall.
Gibson, E. 1978: Understanding the subjective meaning of places. In Ley, D. and Samuels, M. S. (eds.): *Humanistic geography* (Beckenham: Croom Helm) 138-154.
Giddens, A. 1976: *New rules of sociological method*. London: Hutchinson.
—— 1979: *Central problems in social theory*. London: Macmillan.
—— 1981: *A contemporary critique of historical materialism*. London: Macmillan.
Glacken, C. J. 1967: *Traces on the Rhodian shore*. Berkeley: University of California Press.
Godelier, M. 1972: Structure and contradiction in *Capital*. In Blackburn, R. (ed.) *Ideology in social science* (London: Fontana), 334-368.
Golledge, R. G. 1981: Misconceptions, misinterpretations, and misrepresentations of behavioral approaches in human geography. *Environment and Planning A* **13**, 1325-1344.
—— and Amedeo, D. 1968: On laws in geography. *Annals, Association of American Geographers* **58**, 760-774.
Gould, P. R. 1973: On mental maps. In Downs R. M. and Stea D., (eds.) *Image and environment* (London: Edward Arnold), 182-220.
Gould, P. R. 1979: Geography 1957-1977: the Augean period. *Annals Association of American Geographers* **69**, 139-151.
Gregory, D. 1978a: *Ideology, science, and human geography*. London: Hutchinson.
—— 1978b: The discourse of the past: phenomenology, structuralism and historical geography. *Journal of Historical Geography* **4**, 161-173.
—— 1978c: The process of industrial change 1730-1900. In Dodgshon, R. A. and Butlin, R. A. (eds.): *An historical geography of England and Wales* (London: Academic Press), 291-311.
—— 1980: The ideology of control: systems theory and geography. *Tijdschrift voor Economische en Sociale Geographie* **71**, 327-342.
—— 1981: Human agency and human geography. *Transactions, Institute of British Geographers* **NS6**, 1-18.
Grene, M. 1959: *Introduction to existentialism*. Chicago: University of Chicago Press.
Grigg, D. B. 1965: The logic of regional systems. *Annals, Association of American Geographers* **55**, 465-491.
Guelke, L. 1974: An idealist alternative in human geography. *Annals, Association of American Geographers* **64**, 193-202.
—— 1975: On rethinking historical geography. *Area* **7**, 135-138.
—— 1978: Geography and logical positivism. In Herbert, D. T. and Johnston, R. J. (eds.): *Geography and the urban environment* Volume 1 (Chichester: John Wiley), 35-61.
—— 1976: The philosophy of idealism. *Annals, Association of American Geographers* **66**, 168-169.
—— 1982: *Historical understanding in geography*. Cambridge: Cambridge University Press.

Habermas, J. 1972: *Knowledge and human interests*. London: Heinemann.
——1976: *Legitimation crisis*. London: Heinemann.
Hagerstrand, T. 1970: What about people in regional science? *Papers, Regional Science Association* 24, 7–24.
Haggett, P. 1965: *Locational analysis in human geography*. London: Edward Arnold.
——1980: *Human geography: a modern synthesis*. Third Edition. New York: Harper and Row.
Hall, P. (ed.) 1981a: *The inner city*. London: Heinemann.
——1981b: Book review: the limitations of marxist urban studies. *New Society* 57 (982), 439–440.
Hanfling, O. 1981: *Logical positivism*. Oxford: Basil Blackwell.
Harris, C. 1971: Theory and synthesis in historical geography. *Canadian Geographer* 15, 147–172.
——1978: The historical mind and the practice of geography. In Ley, D. and Samuels, M.S. (eds.) *Humanistic geography* (Beckenham: Croom Helm) 123–137.
Harrison, R. T. and Livingstone, D. N. 1982: Understanding in geography: structuring the subjective. In Herbert, D. T. and Johnston, R. J. (eds.) *Geography and the urban environment* Volume 5 (Chichester: John Wiley), 1–40.
Hart, R. A. and Moore, G. T. 1973: The development of spatial cognition: a review. In Downs R. M. and Stea D., (eds.) *Image and Environment* (London: Edward Arnold), 246–287.
Hartshorne, R. 1939: *The nature of geography*. Lancaster, Pa.: The Association of American Geographers.
Harvey, D. 1969: *Explanation in geography*. London: Edward Arnold.
——1973 *Social justice and the city*. London: Edward Arnold.
——1974: Population, resources and the ideology of science. *Economic Geography* 50 256–277.
——1975: Class structure in a capitalist society and the theory of residential differentiation. In Peel, R., Chisholm, M. and Haggett, P. (eds.) *Processes in physical and human geography*. (London: Heinemann), 354–72.
——1978: The urban process under capitalism. *International Journal of Urban and Regional Research* 2, 101–132.
——1981 Marxist geography. In Johnston R. J., (ed.) *The Dictionary of Human Geography* (Oxford: Basil Blackwell) 209–12.
Hay, A. M. 1979: Positivism in human geography: response to critics. In Herbert D. T. and Johnston R. J. (eds.) *Geography and the urban environment* Volume 2 (Chichester: John Wiley), 1–26.
Haynes, R. M. 1975: Dimensional analysis: some applications in human geography. *Geographical Analysis* 7, 51–68.
——1978: A note on dimensions and relationships in human geography. *Geographical Analysis* 10, 288–292.
Heathcote, R. L. 1965: *Back of Bourke*. Melbourne: Melbourne University Press.
Heilbroner, R. L. 1980: *Marxism: for and against*. New York: W. W. Norton.
Held, D. 1980: *Introduction to critical theory* London: Hutchinson.
Hindess, B. 1977: *Philosophy and methodology in the social sciences*. Brighton: Harvester Press.
Hobsbawm, E. J. 1972: Karl Marx's contribution of historiography. In Blackburn, R. (ed.): *Ideology in social science* (London: Fontana), 265–283.
Holland, S. 1976: *Capital versus the regions*. London: Macmillan.
Hoskins, W. G. 1955: *The making of the English landscape*. London: Hodder and Stoughton.

Huggett, R. 1980: *Systems analysis in geography*. Oxford: Oxford University Press.
Hugill, P. J. 1975: Social conduct on the golden mile. *Annals, Association of American Geographers* **65**, 214–228.
Jackson, P. 1981: Phenomenology and social geography. *Area* **13**, 299–305.
James, P. E. and Martin, G. J. 1981: *All possible worlds: a history of geographical ideas*. New York: John Wiley.
Johnston, R. J. 1971: *Urban residential patterns*. London: Bell and Hyman.
—— 1978 *Multivariate Statistical Analysis in Geography*. London: Longman.
—— 1979: *Geography and geographers: Anglo-American human geography since 1945*. London: Edward Arnold.
—— 1980a *City and society*. London: Penguin.
—— 1980b On the nature of explanation in human geography. *Transactions, Institute of British Geographers* **NS5**, 402–412.
—— 1980c: Political geography without politics *Progress in Human Geography* **4**, 439–446.
—— 1980d: *The geography of Federal spending in the United States of America*. Chichester: John Wiley.
—— 1981b Political geography. In Bennett R. J. and Wrigley N., (eds.) *Quantitative geography in Britain: retrospect and prospect* (London: Routledge and Kegan Paul), 374–381.
—— 1981c: The management and autonomy of the local state: the role of the judiciary in the United States *Environment and Planning A* **13**, 1305–1316.
—— 1982a: *The American urban system*. New York: St. Martin's Press.
—— 1982b *Geography and the state*. London: Macmillan.
—— 1982c: On the nature of human geography. *Transactions, Institute of British Geographers* **NS7**,
—— 1982d: Resource analysis, resources management and the integration of human and physical geography. *Progress in Physical Geography*, **6**, 000–000.
—— 1983a: *Geography and geographers: Anglo-American human geography since 1945*. Second edition. London: Edward Arnold.
—— 1983b: Texts, actors and higher managers: judges, bureaucrats, and the political organisation of space *Political Geography Quarterly*, **2**.
—— 1983c: Who needs theory? A response from the schizophrenic middle ground. In Waterman, S. and Kliot, N. (eds.): *Political geography contributions* Beckenham: Croom Helm.
—— and Claval, P. (eds.) 1983: *Geography since the Second World War: an international survey*. Beckenham: Croom Helm.
Jones, D. 1978: Implications of 'schooling' in economic anthropology for interpretations of the economic geography of non-industrial societies. In Berry, B. J. L. (ed.) *The nature of change in geographical ideas*. Northern Illinois University Press, de Kalb, 126–153.
Kaufmann, W. 1975: *Existentialism from Dostoevsky to Sartre*. New York: Meridian Books.
Keat, R. 1981: *The politics of social theory*. Oxford: Basil Blackwell.
—— and Urry, J. 1975 *Social theory as science*. London: Routledge and Kegan Paul.
Keeble, D. E. 1967: Models of economic development. In Chorley, R. J. and Haggett, P. (eds.) *Models in geography*. London: Methuen.
—— 1976: *Industrial location and planning in the United Kingdom*. London: Methuen.
King, L. J. 1976 Alternatives to a positive economic geography. *Annals, Association of American Geographers* **66**, 293–308.
—— 1979 The seventies: disillusionment and consolidation. *Annals, Association of*

American Geographers, **69**, 155-157.
Kirk, W. 1951: Historical geography and the concept of the behavioural environment. *Indian Geographical Journal* **25**, 152-160.
Kirk, W. 1963 Problems of geography. *Geography* **48**, 357-371.
——1978 The road from Mandalay. *Transactions, Institute of British Geographers* **NS3**, 381-394.
Kolakowski, L. 1978: *Main currents of Marxism*. Three volumes. Oxford: Clarendon Press.
Kraft, V. 1953 *The Vienna circle: the origin of neo-positivism*. New York: Philosophical Library.
Kuhn, T. S. 1962: *The structure of scientific revolutions*. Chicago: University of Chicago Press.
Kurzweil, E. 1980: *The age of structuralism*. New York: Columbia University Press.
Lacey, A. R. 1976: *A dictionary of philosophy*. London: Routledge and Kegan Paul.
Larrain, J. 1979: *The concept of ideology*. London: Hutchinson.
Leach, E. R. 1974 *Lévi-Strauss*. London: Fontana.
——1981 British social anthropology and Lévi-Straussian structuralism. In Blau, P. M. and Merton, R. K. (eds.) *Continuities in structural enquiry* (Beverly Hills: Sage Publications), 27-50.
Leonard, S. 1982: Urban managerialism. *Progress in Human Geography* **6** (London: Edward Arnold), 190-215.
Lewis, G. M. 1981: Amerindian antecedents of American academic geography. In Blouet, B. W. (ed.): *The origins of academic geography in the United States* (Conn.: Archon Books Hamden,), 19-36.
Lewis, J. and Melville, B. 1978: The politics of epistemology in regional science. *London Papers in Regional Science* **8** (London: Pion), 82-100.
Lewis, P. F. 1979 Axioms for reading the landscape. In Meinig, D. W. (ed.) *The interpretation of ordinary landscapes* (New York: Oxford University Press), 11-32.
Lewis, P. W. 1965: Three related problems in the formulation of laws in geography. *The Professional Geographer* **17(5)**, 24-27.
Ley, D. 1974: *The black inner city as frontier outpost*. Washington DC: Association of American Geographers.
——1977: Social geography and the taken-for-granted world. *Transactions, Institute of British Geographers* **NS2**, 498-512.
——1978: Social geography and social action. In Ley, D. and Samuels, M. S. (eds.): *Humanistic geography* (London: Croom Helm), 41-57.
——1980: *Geography without man: a humanistic critique*. Oxford: Research Paper 24, School of Geography, University of Oxford.
——1981: Behavioral geography and the philosophies of meaning. In Cox, K. R. and Golledge, R. G. (eds.) *Behavioral problems in geography revisited* (London: Methuen), 209-30.
——and Samuels, M.S. 1978: Introduction: concepts of modern humanism in geography. In Ley, D. and Samuels, M. S. (eds.): *Humanistic geography* (Beckenham: Croom Helm), 1-18.
Livingstone, D. N. and Harrison, R. T. 1981: Immanuel Kant, subjectivism, and human geography: a preliminary investigation. *Transactions, Institute of British Geographers* **NS6**, 359-374.
Lloyd, P. E. and Dicken, P. 1978: *Location in space*. London: Harper and Row.
Lowenthal, D. (1961) Geography, experience and imagination: towards a geographical epistemology. *Annals, Association of American Geographers* **51**, 241-260.

——1975a: Past time, present place: landscape and memory. *Geographical Review* **65**, 1–36.
——1975b The place of the past in the American landscape. In Lowenthal, D. and Bowden, M. J. (eds.) *Geographies of the mind* (New York: Oxford University Press), 89–118.
Lowenthal, D. and Prince, H. C. 1964: The English landscape. *Geographical Review* **54**, 309–346.
Lynch, K. 1960: *The image of the city.* Cambridge, Mass.: MIT Press.
Lyons, J. 1977: *Chomsky.* London: Fontana.
Macquarrie, J. 1972: *Existentialism.* London: Hutchinson.
Magee, B. 1973: *Popper.* London: Fontana.
Martensson, S. 1979: *On the formation of biographies.* Lund: CWK Gleerup.
Martin, R. L. and Oeppen, J. E. 1975: The identification of regional forecasting models using space-time correlation functions. *Transactions, Institute of British Geographers* **66**, 95–118.
Marx, K. 1976: *Capital.* London: Penguin.
Massey, D. 1979: A critical evaluation of industrial-location theory. In Hamilton, F. E. I. and Linge, G. J. R. (eds.) *Spatial analysis, industry and the industrial environment* (Chichester: John Wiley), 57–72.
——and Meegan, R. A. 1979: The geography of industrial reorganisation. *Progress in Planning* **10**, 155–237.
Mercer, D. C. and Powell, J. M. 1972: *Phenomenology and related non-positivistic viewpoints in the social sciences.* Clayton, Victoria: Monash Publications in Geography 1.
Mikesell, M. W. 1978: Tradition and innovation in cultural geography. *Annals, Association of American Geographers* **68**, 1–16.
Morris, D. 1967: *The naked ape* London: Jonathan Cape.
Muir, R. 1978: Radical geography or a new orthodoxy? *Area* **10**, 322–327.
——1979 Radical geography and Marxism. *Area* **11**, 126–127.
Mulkay, M. J. 1975: Three models of scientific development. *Sociological Review* **23**, 509–526.
Nell, E. 1972: Economics: the revival of political economy. In Blackburn, R. (ed.) *Ideology in social science* (London: Fontana), 76–95.
Newman, J. L. 1973: The use of the term 'hypothesis' in geography. *Annals, Association of American Geographers* **63**, 22–27.
Nystuen, J. D. 1963: Identification of some fundamental spatial concepts. *Papers of the Michigan Academy of Science, Arts and Letters* **48**, 373–384.
Olafson, F. A. 1967: *Principles and persons.* Baltimore: The Johns Hopkins Press.
Olsson, G. 1975: *Bird in egg.* Ann Arbor: Department of Geography, University of Michigan; London: Pion.
——1978: Of ambiguity or far cries from a memorializing mamafesta. In Ley, D. and Samuels, M. S. (eds.): *Humanistic geography* (Beckenham: Croom Helm), 109–120.
——1979 Social science and human action or on hitting your head against the ceiling of language. In Gale, S. and Olsson, G. (eds.) *Philosophy in geography* (Dordrecht: Reidel) 287–308.
Openshaw, S. and Taylor, P. J. 1980: A million or so correlation coefficients: three experiments on the modifiable areal unit problem. In Wrigley, N. (ed.) *Statistical applications in the spatial sciences* (London: Pion), 127–144.
Outhwaite, W. 1975: *Understanding of social life: the method called verstehen.* London: George Allen and Unwin.
Passmore, J. 1957: Logical positivism. In Edwards, P. (ed.) *Encyclopedia of philo-*

sophy (New York: Macmillan), 414–419.
Peet, J. R. 1975: Inequality and poverty: a Marxist-geographic theory. *Annals, Association of American Geographers* **65** 564–571.
——1977: The development of radical geography in the United States. *Progress in Human Geography* **1**, 64–87.
Piaget, J. 1971: *Structuralism*. London: Routledge and Kegan Paul.
——and Lyons, J. V. 1981: Marxism: dialectical materialism, social formation and the geographic relations. In Harvey, M. E. and Holly, B. P. (eds.) *Themes in geographic thought* (Beckenham: Croom Helm), 187–205.
Penning-Rowsell, E. C. 1981: Fluctuating fortunes in gauging landscape value. *Progress in Human Geography* **5**, 25–41.
Pocock, D. C. D. 1981a: Place and the novelist. *Transactions, Institute of British Geograpers* **NS6**, 337–347.
——1981b: Introduction: imaginative literature and the geographer. In Pocock D. C. D. (ed.) *Humanistic geography and literature* (Beckenham: Croom Helm), 9–19.
Pooler, J. A. 1977: The origins of the spatial tradition in geography: an interpretation. *Ontario Geography* **11**, 56–83.
Popper, K. R. 1945 *The open society and its enemies*. London: Routledge and Kegan Paul.
——1972: *Conjectures and refutations*. Fourth edition. London: Routledge and Kegan Paul.
——1976: *Unended quest*. London: Fontana.
Powell, J. M. 1970: *The public lands of Australia Felix* (Melbourne: Oxford University Press).
——1971: Utopia, millenium and the cooperative ideal. *The Australian Geographer* **11**, 606–618.
——1977: *Mirrors of the new world*. Folkestone: Dawson.
——1980: The haunting of Saloman's house: geography and the limits of science. *The Australian Geographer* **14**, 327–341.
Pred, A. R. 1967: *Behavior and location: foundations for a geographic and dynamic location theory*. Lund: CWK Gleerup.
——1977a: *City-systems in advanced economies*. London: Hutchinson.
——1977b: The choreography of existence: comments on Hagerstrand's time-geography and its usefulness. *Economic Geography* **53**, 207–221.
——1979: The academic past through a time-geographic looking glass. *Annals, Association of American Geographers* **69**, 175–180.
——1981a: Social reproduction and the time-geography of everyday life. *Geografiska Annaler* **63B**, 5–22.
——1981b: Production, family, and free-time projects: a time-geographic perspective on the individual and societal change in nineteenth century U.S. cities. *Journal of Historical Geography* **7**, 3–36.
Prince, H. C. 1971: Real, imagined and abstract worlds of the past. In Board, C. et al. (eds.) *Progress in Geography 3* (London: Edward Arnold,), 1–86.
Quaini, M. 1982: *Geography and Marxism*. Oxford: Basil Blackwell.
Relph, E. 1970: An inquiry into the relations between phenomenology and geography. *Canadian Geographer* **14**, 193–201.
——1976: *Place and placelessness*. London: Pion.
——1981a: *Rational landscapes and humanistic geography*. Beckenham: Croom Helm.
——1981b *Phenomenology*. In Harvey, M. E. and Holly, B. P. (eds.) *Themes in geographic thought*. (Beckenham: Croom Helm), 99–114.
Rieser, R. 1973: The territorial illusion and behavioural sink: critical notes on

behavioural geography. *Antipode* **5(3)**, 52–57.
Rose, C. 1980: Human geography as text interpretation. In Buttimer, A. and Seamon, D. (eds.) *The human experience of space and place* (Beckenham: Croom Helm), 123–134.
——1981: Wilhelm Dilthey's philosophy of historical understanding. In Stoddart, D. R. (ed.): *Geography, ideology and social concern* (Oxford: Basil Blackwell), 99–133.
Rossi, I. 1981: Transformational structuralism: Lévi-Strauss's definition of social structure. In Blau, P. M. and Merton R. K. (eds.) *Continuities in structural inquiry* (Beverly Hills: Sage Publications), 51–80.
Rowles, G. 1978: Reflections on experiential field work. In Ley, D. and Samuels, M. S. (eds.) *Humanistic geography* (Beckenham: Croom Helm), 173–193.
Rudner, R. B. 1966: *Philosophy of social science*. Englewood Cliffs; Prentice-Hall.
Sack, R. D 1974 The spatial separatist theme in geography. *Economic Geography* **50**, 1–19.
——1980a: Conceptions of geographic space. *Progress in Human Geography* **4**, 313–345.
——1980b: *Conceptions of space in social thought*. London: Macmillan.
Samuels, M. S. 1978a: Existentialism and human geography. In Ley, D. and Samuels, M. S. (eds.) *Humanistic geography* (Beckenham: Croom Helm), 22–40.
——1978b: Individual and landscape: thoughts on China and the Tao of Mao. In Ley, D. and Samuels, M. S. (eds.) *Humanistic geography* (Beckenham: Croom Helm), 283–296.
——1979: The biography of landscape. In Meinig, D. W. (ed.) *The interpretation of ordinary landscapes* (New York: Oxford University Press), 51–80.
——1981: An existential geography. In Harvey, M. E. and Holly, B. P. (eds.) *Themes in geographic thought* (Beckenham: Croom Helm), 115–133.
Santos, M. 1975: *The shared space* London: Methuen.
Sauer, C. O. 1925: *The morphology of landscape*. Berkeley: University of California Publications in Geography **2**, 19–54.
Saunders, P. 1981: *Social theory and the urban question*. London: Hutchinson.
Saussure, de. F. 1966: *Course in general linguistics*. New York: McGraw Hill.
Sayer, D. 1979: *Marx's method*. Brighton: Harvester Press.
Sayer, R. A. 1979a: Epistemology and conceptions of people and nature in geography. *Geoforum* **10**, 19–44.
——1979b: Understanding urban models versus understanding cities. *Environment and Planning A* **11**, 853–862.
——1982: Explanation in economic geography: abstraction versus generalization. *Progress in Human Geography*, **6**, 68–88.
Scheibling, J. 1977: Debates et combats sur la crise de la geographie. *La Pensée* **194**, 41–56.
Schutz, A. 1964: *Collected papers II: studies in social theory*. The Hague: Martinus Nijhoff.
——A. 1971: *Collected Papers I: the problem of social reality*. The Hague: Martinus Nijhoff.
——A. 1972: *The phenomenology of the social world*. Translated by G. Walsh and F. Lehnert. London: Heinemann. First German edition 1932.
Seamon, D. 1979: *A geography of the lifeworld*. London: Croom Helm.
Sensat, J. 1979: *Habermas and Marxism*. Beverly Hills: Sage Publications.
Shaw, W. H. 1978: *Marx's theory of history*. London: Hutchinson.
Silk, J. 1982: Commentary on 'On the nature of explanation in human geography'. *Transactions, Institute of British Geographers* **NS7**, 380–84.

Slater, D. 1973: The poverty of modern geographical enquiry. *Pacific Viewpoint* **16**, 159-176.
Smart, B. 1976: *Sociology, phenomenology and marxian analysis*. London: Routledge and Kegan Paul.
Smith, D. M. 1977: *Human geography: a welfare approach*. London: Edward Arnold.
Smith, D. M. 1979: Modelling industrial location. In Hamilton, F. E. I. and Linge, G. J. R. (eds.) *Spatial analysis, industry and the industrial environment* (Chichester: John Wiley), 37-55.
——1981: Marxian economics. In Johnston, R. J., (ed.) *The Dictionary of Human Geography* (Oxford: Basil Blackwell), 203-9.
——1981b: *Industrial location: an economic geographical analysis*. New York: John Wiley.
Smith, N. 1979: Geography, science and post-positivist modes of explanation. *Progress in Human Geography* **3**, 356-383.
Smith, N. and Wilson, D. 1979a: *Modern linguistics: the results of Chomsky's revolution*. London: Penguin.
Smith, S. J. 1981: Humanistic method in contemporary social geography. *Area* **13**, 293-298.
Soja, E. W. 1980: The socio-spatial dialectic. *Annals, Association of American Geographers* **70**, 207-225.
——and Hadjimichalis, C. 1979: Between geographical materialism and spatial fetishism: some observations on the development of Marxist spatial analysis. *Antipode* **11(3)**, 3-11.
Spiegelberg, H. 1975: *Doing phenomenology*. The Hague: Martinus Nijhoff.
——1976 *The phenomenological movement: a historical introduction*. Second edition; two volumes. The Hague: Martinus Nijhoff.
Stoddart, D. R. 1966: Darwin's impact on geography. *Annals, Association of American Geographers* **56**, 683-98.
Storper, M., Walker, R. A., Widess, E. (1981) Performance regulation and industrial location: a case study. *Environment and Planning A*, **13**, 321-338.
Taylor, P. J. 1977: *Quantitative methods in geography: an introduction to spatial analysis*. New York: Houghton Mifflin.
——1981: Factor analysis in geographical research. In Bennett, R. J. (ed.) *European Progress in Spatial Analysis*. (London: Pion), 251-267.
——1982: A materialist framework for political geography. *Transactions, Institute of British Geographers* **NS7**, 15-34.
——1983: The question of theory in political geography. In Waterman, S. and Kliot, N. (eds.) *Political geography contributions*. Beckenham: Croom Helm.
——and Johnston, R. J. 1979: *Geography of elections*. London: Penguin.
Thomas, D. 1979 *Naturalism and social science*. Cambridge: Cambridge University Press.
Thrift, N. J. 1979 Unemployment in the inner city: urban problem or structural imperative? In Herbert, D. T. and Johnston, R. J. (eds.) *Geography and the urban environment* Volume 2 (Chichester: John Wiley) 125-226.
Timms, D. W. G. 1971: *The urban mosaic*. Cambridge: Cambridge University Press.
Tocalis, T. R. 1978: Changing theoretical foundations of the gravity concept of human interaction. In Berry, B. J. L. (ed.) *The nature of change in geographical ideas* (de Kalb: Northern Illinois University Press.), 65-124.
Tuan, Y-F 1974a: Space and place: humanistic perspectives. In C. Board et al.

(eds.) *Progress in Geography 6* (London: Edward Arnold), 211-252.
—— 1974b: *Topophilia*. Englewood Cliffs: Prentice-Hall.
—— 1976: Humanistic geography. *Annals, Association of American Geographers* **66**, 266-276.
—— 1977: *Space and place*. London: Edward Arnold.
—— 1978: Literature and geography: implications for geographical research. In Ley, D. and Samuels, M. S. (eds.) *Humanistic geography* (Beckenham: Croom Helm.), 194-206.
—— 1979: *Landscapes of fear*. Oxford: Basil Blackwell.
Urry, J. 1981: Localities, regions and social class. *International Journal of Urban and Regional Research* **5** 455-474.
Walker, R. A 1978: The transformation of urban structure in the nineteenth century and the beginnings of suburbanization. In Cox, K. R. (ed.) *Urbanization and conflict in market societies* (Chicago: Maaroufa Press), 165-212.
Walker, R. A. 1981a: A theory of suburbanization: capitalism and the construction of space in the United States. In Dear, M. J. and Scott, A. J. (eds.) *Urbanization and urban planning in capitalist society* (London: Methuen), 383-430.
—— 1981b: Left-wing libertarianism, an academic disorder: a response to David Sibley. *The Professional Geographer* **33** 5-9.
Wallace, I. 1978: Towards a humanized conception of economic geography. In Ley. D. and Samuels, M. S. (eds.) *Humanistic geography* (Beckenham: Croom Helm), 91-108.
Williams, P. 1982: Restructuring urban managerialism: towards a political economy of urban allocation. *Environment and Planning A* **14**, 95-106.
Wilson, A. G. 1970: *Entropy in urban and regional modelling*. London: Pion.
—— 1981: *Catastrophe theory and bifurcation*. Beckenham: Croom Helm.
Wolff, K. H. 1979: Phenomenology and sociology. In Bottomore T. and Nisbet R. (eds.) *A history of sociological analysis* (London: Heinemann), 498-556.
Wooldridge, S. W. 1936: The Anglo-Saxon settlement. In Darby, H. C. (ed.) *An historical geography of England before 1500* (Cambridge: Cambridge University Press), 88-132.
Wright, J. K. 1947: *Terrae incognitae*: the place of imagination in geography. *Geographical Review* **37**, 1-15.

General index

agency 102, 103-5, 113
alienation 66, 92-3, 95
Althusser, L. 92
anarchism 107
autocorrelation 40

behavioural environment 68-9
behavioural geography 36-8, 72, 79
behaviourism 26, 75, 114
bracketing 56, 58, 60, 130

capitalism 92-9, 100, 122, 114-6, 132-3
central place theory 32-3, 37, 43
Christaller, W. 32
Chomsky, N. 88
coherence 53-5
Collingwood, R. G. 54-6
Comte, A. 11-12, 25, 29, 46
consciousness 57, 58, 61, 75, 80-1, 84, 89, 91
core-periphery 115-6
critical theory (science) 105-7, 110, 130, 131, 133

development 114-6
dialectics 95-7, 100, 102, 105, 111-2, 116, 119
diffusion 35, 44
Dilthey, W. 61, 72
direct realism 26
discipline 1-2, 24-5, 28-31, 83, 110-1, 121, 123

eclecticism 130
ecology 34
economic geography 9, 43, 109, 114-6
eiconics 77
electoral geography 118
emancipation 105-7
empiricism 4, 6, 28, 47, 49, 58

entitiation 40
environmental determinism 7
epistemology 4, 19, 31, 122, 128
epoché 60
essence 65-7, 91
ethology 80
ethnomethodology 64-5, 72
everyday world 82-3
exceptionalism 28
existentialism 65-7, 69, 73, 77

falsification 14, 16, 22
Frankfurt school 105-7
functionalism 26

geology 28
geosophy 68

Habermas, J. 105-7
habitat theory 81
Hegel, G. 95
Heidegger, M. 65
hermeneutic 57, 60-1, 64-5, 72-3, 84, 106, 127, 133
historical geography 8-9, 68, 70-1, 76-8, 119-20
historical materialism 92-9, 100, 110-1
history 54-6, 70, 78, 89, 98, 131
Hoover, E. M. 33
human geography 2-10
humanistic 5, 52-86, 104, 122
Husserl, E. 56, 58, 60, 61, 71, 82
hypothesis 14, 15, 16-17, 18-25, 30, 48

idealism 52-6, 70-1, 102
ideal types 63-4
ideology 124, 126-7, 128
individual 39-41
induction 20-1, 37
industrial location theory 33-4, 114

148 *General index*

inner-city problem 115–6
instrumentalism 44, 47, 134
intentionality 57
intersubjectivity 59
interpretive sociology 63–4

Kropotkin, P. 107

landscape 73, 77, 81–3, 119
land use 33, 117
language 85, 106
law 17, 19, 20–29, 30, 32, 47–9, 101–3, 109, 125
learning 91
Lefebvre, H. 111
Lévi-Strauss, C. 88–91, 107
life-world 58, 59, 60, 63
linguistics 88–9
literature 79
logical positivism 12–18, 46–56, 128
Losch, A. 32

Mackinder, H. J. 118
managerialism 118, 132–3
Marxism 67, 91–107, 108–20, 125–6, 127, 130, 133
metaphor 122–3
metaphysics 13–4
methodology 4–5, 18–25, 30–1, 55–6, 58–9, 67, 74–5, 82, 89–90, 122
model 21, 24–5, 29, 30, 49

naturalism 26, 125
normative 36

ontology 4, 31, 68, 122
organism 7, 41

perception 69
phenomenal environment 68–9
phenomenology 56–65, 67, 68, 71–2, 74–5, 78, 84, 125, 127, 128
philosophy 2, 4–6
physical geography 3, 41–2
Piaget, J. 90–1, 107–8
place ballet 82
placelessness 78
political geography 8, 49, 118–9, 132–3
positivism 5, 11–25
    in social science 25–31

in human geography 28–50, 72, 74, 79, 122
probability 22–4
psychologism 125

quantification – see statistics

realism, direct 26
    transcendental 76, 101–3, 113
Reclus, E. 107
reductionism 124–5
regional geography 5–6, 7–8, 70
regionalism 6–7, 32
regional problem 115–6
regional science 32, 34
religion 66–7
Ricardo, D. 93
Rostow, W. 114

Sartre, J-P 65, 66
scientific method 13, 18–25
scientific politics 13, 18, 28, 47, 125
scientism 13, 18, 28, 30, 46
segregation 116–8
sense of place 78–81
social areas 34, 116–8
social engineering 26
social geography 8, 109, 116–8
social science 3–4, 24–31, 100, 102, 123–4
spatial interaction 34–5, 37
spatial science 36, 44–5
state 118–9, 132–3
statistics 22–4, 28–9, 35, 38–9, 40–1, 46, 47–50, 112, 131, 128, 130, 188
structuralism 5, 87–121
structural-functionalism 45–87
structure as construct 88–91, 107–8
structure as process 91–107, 108–14
structuration 83, 103–5, 111, 119–20, 131–2
suburbanization 118
surplus value 93–4
systems 41–6, 103, 125
systematic geography 7–8

taken-for-granted world 62–3, 71–2, 78
tautology 14
territoriality 80–1
theory 24–5, 30, 46–50, 53–6, 71, 100
time geography 83–4, 119–20

Index to authors

Abler, R. F. 35, 114, 127
Adams, J. S. 35, 114, 127
Agnew, J. A. 74
Amedeo, D. 29
Andreski, S. 11, 12
Appleton, J. 81
Archer, J. C. 132, 133
Ardrey, R. 80
Asheim, B. T. 109, 111
Ayer, A. J. 13, 14, 15, 38

Ballabon, M. B. 30
Barnes, B. 24
Bassett, K. 116, 118
Bauman, Z. 60, 64
Beavon, K. S. O. 33
Bennett, R. J. 41, 42, 43, 44, 45, 47, 48, 49, 125
Berry, B. J. L. 33, 118, 130
Bhaskar, R. 101, 102, 113
Billinge, M. 71, 74, 123
Blaut, J. M. 108, 119
Blouet, B. W. 108
Boden, M. A. 91
Bordessa, R. 113
Bottomore, T. 97
Braithwaite, R. B. 17, 19, 20
Breitbart, M. M. 107
Brewer, A. 114
Brookfield, H. C. 114
Brown, R. H. 68
Bunting, T. E. 37, 46
Bunge, W. 113
Burnett, A. D. 118
Burton, I. 29
Butlin, R. A. 119
Buttimer, A. 69, 73

Carlstein, T. 84
Caro, R. A. 77

Castells, M. 118
Chapman, G.P. 40, 45
Chisholm, M. 33, 42, 126
Chorley, R. J. 21, 29, 41, 42, 43, 125
Clark, G. L. 119
Claval, P. 8
Cliff, A. D. 35, 40
Collingwood, R. G. 54, 55, 56
Cox, K. R. 3, 32, 72, 113, 118
Cybriwsky, R.A. 83

Dear, M. J. 119, 125
Dicken, P. 34
Downs, R. M. 108
Dunbar, G. S. 107
Duncan, J. S. 74, 79
Duncan, S. S. 114, 126
Dunford, M. F. 110, 111

Eliot Hurst, M. E. 110
Entrikin, J. N. 57, 75, 84
Ewing, A. C. 52, 53
Eyles, J. 117, 130

Faber, M. 56
Flew, A. 14
Freeman, T. W. 6, 8

Garfinkel, H. 64
Gibson, E. 71
Giddens, A. 59, 60, 61, 64, 92, 103, 104, 105, 119, 132
Glacken, C. J. 81
Godelier, M. 98
Golledge, R.G. 29, 36, 37, 38, 46, 47, 108
Gould, P.R. 8, 28, 35, 108, 114, 127
Gregory, D. 11, 44, 46, 47, 84, 89, 103, 105, 107, 111, 113, 119, 123, 125, 130, 133
Grene, M. 65, 66

uneven development 114–5
urban geography 8–9, 71, 116–8

value-freedom 13, 18, 28, 130
verification 14–6, 22–4, 38–9, 99
verstehen 56, 61, 64, 68

Vienna school 12, 14–5, 16, 30
von Thunen, J. H. 33

Wallerstein, I. 119
Weber, A. 33
Weber, M. 62, 83
welfare geography 9

Index to authors

Grigg, D. B. 29
Guelke, L. 37, 40, 70, 71, 75

Habermas, J. 11, 106
Hagerstrand, T. 83, 84
Haggett, P. 3, 21, 29, 35
Hall, P. 116, 120, 125
Hanfling, O. 12, 15, 18
Harris, C. 70, 74
Harrison, R. T. 20, 122, 129
Hart, R. A. 108
Hartshorne, R. 7, 28
Harvey, D. 30, 31, 38, 41, 42, 46, 109, 110, 112, 113, 116, 117, 118, 120, 123, 133
Hay, A. M. 14, 16, 123, 361, 129
Haynes, R. M. 36
Heathcote, R. L. 76
Heilbroner, R. L. 95
Held, D. 106, 107
Hindess, B. 123
Hobsbawm, E. J. 98
Holland, S. 116
Hoskins, W. G. 77
Huggett, R. 42
Hugill, P. J. 79

Jackson, P. 68, 73
James, P. E. 2
Johnston, R. J. 3, 5, 8, 28, 36, 40, 48, 49, 81, 107, 109, 115, 116, 118, 119, 122, 123, 130, 131, 132, 133
Jones, D. 107

Kaufmann, W. 65
Keat, R. 13, 18, 28, 47, 51, 101, 102, 123, 124, 125, 129
Keeble, D. E. 48, 114
King, L. J. 125
Kirk, W. 68, 69
Kolakowski, L. 91, 93, 95, 97, 98, 99, 100, 105
Kraft, V 12
Kuhn, T. S. 24
Kurzweil, E. 89, 90, 92, 111

Lacey, A. R. 11, 13, 21
Larrain, J. 124
Lee, R. 130
Leonard, S. 118, 132
Lewis, G. M. 108
Lewis, J. 113

Lewis, P. W. 29
Ley, D. 69, 72, 82, 83, 124, 126, 127
Livingstone, D. N. 20, 122, 129
Lloyd, P. E. 34
Lowenthal, D. 69, 71, 77, 78, 81
Lynch, K. 79
Lyons, J. 88
Lyons, J. V. 109, 110

McCarthy, J. J. 113
McCleary, G. F. 108
Macquarie, J. 66, 67
Magee, B. 16
Martensson, S. 83
Martin, G. J. 2
Martin, R. L. 45, 123
Marx, K. 105
Massey, D. 114
Meegan, R. A. 114
Melville, B. 113
Mercer, D. C. 71, 72, 75
Mikesell, M. W. 107
Moore, G. T. 108
Morris, D. 80
Muir, R. 126
Mulkay, M. J. 17, 18

Nell, E. 100
Nystuen, J. D. 32

Oeppen, J. 45
Olafson, F. A. 66
Olsson, G. 85
Openshaw, S. 40
Ord, J. K. 40
Outhwaite, W. 61

Parkes, D. N. 84
Passmore, J. 49
Peet, J. R. 108, 109, 110, 112
Penning-Rowsell, E. C. 81
Piaget, J. 90, 91
Pocock, D. C. D. 79
Pooler, J. A. 32
Popper, K. R. 16, 95, 100
Powell, J. M. 71, 72, 75, 76, 77, 120
Pred, A. R. 36, 43, 83, 84, 85, 119, 120, 131
Prince, H. C. 76, 77, 81

Quaini, M. 112, 119

Relph, E. 68, 71, 72, 74, 78
Rieser, R. 125
Rose, C. 72, 77
Rossi, I. 87, 89
Rowles, G. D. 75
Rudner, R. G. 50

Sack, R. D. 36, 79, 80
Samuels, M. S. 69, 73, 74, 127
Santos, M. 115
Sauer, C. O. 68, 70
Saunders, P. 99, 116
Sayer, D. 99
Sayer, R. A. 112, 113, 125, 126, 129, 131
Scheibling, J. A. 111
Schutz, A. 62, 63
Scott, A. J. 125
Seamon, D. 80, 82, 83
Sensat, J. 106
Shaw, W. H. 94, 95, 96, 100
Short, J. R. 116, 118
Silk, J. 130
Slater, D. 37
Smart, B. 127
Smith, D. M. 9, 34, 93, 109
Smith, N. 114

Smith S. J. 72
Soja, E. W. 111, 112, 114
Spiegelberg, H. 56, 57, 58, 59, 82
Stea, D. 108
Stoddart, D. R. 7, 9, 28
Storper, M. 115

Taylor, P. J. 35, 40, 48, 49, 118, 119, 131, 132, 133
Thomas, D. 26, 27
Thrift, N. J. 84, 116
Timms, D. W. G. 34
Tocalis, T. R. 34
Tuan, Y-F 69, 78, 81, 82, 127

Urry, J. R. 101, 102, 119, 123, 124, 125

Walker, R. A. 115, 118, 128, 131
Wallace, I. 75
Widess, E. 115
Williams, P. 135
Wilson, A. G. 45
Wolff, K. H. 56
Wooldridge, S.W. 68
Wright, J. K. 68
Wrigley, N. 47